A CAPACITY TO PUNISH

A CAPACITY TO PUNISH

The Ecology of Crime and Punishment

HENRY N. PONTELL

Indiana University Press • Bloomington

Part of this work
the Law Enforcement Assistance Administration, U.S. Department of
Justice. Researchers undertaking such projects under Government spon-
sorship are encouraged to express freely their professional judgment.
Therefore, points of view or opinions stated do not necessarily
represent the official position or policy of the U.S. Department
of Justice.

Copyright © 1984 by Henry N. Pontell

Manufactured in the United States of America

Library of Congress Cataloging in Publication Data
Pontell, Henry N., 1950–
  A capacity to punish.
  Bibliography: p.
  Includes index.
  1. Criminal justice, Administration of—United
States.   2. Crime and criminals—United States.
3. Punishment—United States.   4. Crime prevention—
United States.   I. Title.
HV9471.P66   1984   364'.973   83-48107
ISBN 0-253-31309-0
1   2   3   4   5   88   87   86   85   84

In memory of my mother,
Barbara ("Bobbie") Pontell

CONTENTS

Figures

Tables

PREFACE

This book is certainly not the first to be written about crime and punishment, nor will it likely be the last. The topics of deterrence and crime control have been studied for quite some time, and it is extremely doubtful that they will soon disappear as major areas of scientific research or public interest. A primary reason for this, I suspect, is that the issues surrounding these topics are highly complex in nature and touch on important theoretical and policy questions that provide for much debate and controversy in both scientific and public spheres. It is my hope that this book will add to the controversy surrounding crime and punishment, and, in the process, provide some new ideas for further research.

The research presented here derives from my doctoral studies in sociology at the State University of New York at Stony Brook. My teachers and fellow students there provided a learning environment that was rarely dull, and often quite stimulating. Among the more talented professors in the sociology department was Forrest ("Woody") Dill, who planted the seed from which this study grew. He showed great interest in my work and was instrumental in my receiving a U.S. Department of Justice fellowship, which largely supported this research. Woody always offered interesting ideas, and our discussions resulted in the term "system capacity," which is a central focus of this book. Woody was an excellent advisor and was asked to serve on a number of doctoral student committees during his years at Stony Brook. He was always there when I needed advice, was my best critic, and was a thoughtful scholar who had a great command of the sociological and criminological literature. Woody left Stony Brook in 1978 to assume a faculty position in sociology at the University of California, Davis. In August 1981, Woody was killed in a car crash near the university. He was a very close colleague to whom I will always be grateful.

Many other people have helped shape this work. Hanan Selvin graciously accepted the chair of my doctoral committee upon Woody's departure from Stony Brook, and has shown great interest in my work since we met in 1973. I am most appreciative of his fine guidance and detailed comments on my writing. Michael Schwartz has also had a great impact on my research, and was largely responsible for my pursuing graduate study. Michael's pointed criticisms, wise conceptualizations, and unbounded enthusiasm have been a great inspiration to me. I also thank Peter Williams, whose knowledge of the philosophy of law provided informative discussions that helped to form many ideas in this study. I am also indebted to William Atwood, whose computer expertise was invaluable.

xi

While visiting the Center for the Study of Law and Society at the University of California, Berkeley in 1976, I had numerous and productive discussions with Sheldon Messinger, Martin Forst, and Pamela Utz. Rod Watanabe made it very easy for me to get things done while visiting the Center. I accomplished more during that short visit than I could have ever imagined, and I greatly appreciate their efforts on my behalf. I also thank Floyd Feeney of the University of California, Davis, School of Law, and numerous officials of the Bureau of Criminal Statistics and Special Services and of the Bureau of Finance for their help in providing the data used in this study.

After continuing my work at the University of California, Irvine, I have greatly benefited from comments made by new colleagues, including Paul Jesilow, John Braithwaite, Gilbert Geis, Joseph DiMento, Arnold Binder, Peter Scharf, John Dombrink, James Meeker, Harold Pepinsky, David Biles, and Mark Baldassare.

I also thank Joan Gordon of the Program in Social Ecology, and Doris McBride and the staff of the Public Policy Research Organization, University of California, Irvine, for their assistance in preparing the manuscript, and my research assistant, Mary Jane O'Brien, for her help in assembling the notes and bibliography.

Finally, I owe a special debt to my parents, Barbara and Bernard, my sisters, Mina and Lisa, my wife, Michelle, and our daughter, Lilli, without whose love, encouragement, and support this book would never have been written.

A CAPACITY TO PUNISH

I. Introduction

> It is hardly possible for any legal machinery to do all which our volu-
> minous penal legislation expects of it. Even lawyers scarcely appreciate
> the operation of the limitations upon all effective legal action. Thus
> there is constant pressure upon the law to "do something" whether it
> may do anything worthwhile or not. In periods of transition or expan-
> sion, the tendency is especially strong to call upon the law to do more
> than it is adapted to do. The result is sure to be failure, and failure
> affects the whole legal order injuriously.[1]

When the criminal justice system grows, so does the crime problem.
The expansion of the criminal justice apparatus is a result of both
public and legislative reactions to crime. At the same time, however,
the criminal justice system itself produces the official data that defines
what we know as the "crime problem." A larger system allows greater
opportunities for crime to be officially recorded. In turn, we react to
such data by further increasing the state's social control mechanism—
the criminal justice system.

We typically rely on the criminal justice system to do more than it is
capable of doing. In the process, we have increased the size of the
criminal justice system and have at the same time witnessed a growth
in criminal behavior. Creating more laws and legislating harsher punishments have not solved the "crime problem." It is the purpose of
this book to show why this is the case, and, in doing so, to demonstrate
that increased government expenditures that aim at criminal deterrence are futile given the social conditions that breed crime.

The control of crime remains one of the most important social
issues of our time. We are constantly confronted with news of what
appears to most as antisocial, and sometimes even inhuman, forms of
behavior. The cost of such illegal activity is great, not only in terms of
losses to taxpayers and crime victims, but in what it does to us men-
tally as a nation. People are scared, whether or not they have real

1

reason to be. Ours is a society marked by increasing suspicion, anxiety, and paranoia over the fear of being criminally victimized. This is true especially for the elderly and the poor, the most vulnerable portions of the population, who must bear the brunt of the ugliest crimes. Our fears are brought about through reported crime rates, which are themselves partially created by official agencies. Ironically, our response to the perceived crime problem is to further increase resources, which keeps the cycle intact.

What became known in the 1960s as the war against crime continues into the 1980s, although the nature of the movement has changed significantly. The liberal vision of reducing crime by attacking its social causes, the so-called roots of crime, was replaced in the 1970s by a more "pragmatic" and conservative ideology that aimed at punishing criminals and largely ignored the role of the social system in generating crime. The all-out "war" was transformed into a battle between the forces of good and evil.

Social programs designed to attack the social roots of crime and to rehabilitate offenders did not produce conclusive results in the eyes of some researchers and policy makers. Increased expenditures in criminal justice and the community were accompanied by higher reported crime, leading many to question the effectiveness of community-based programs designed to prevent criminal activity. As far as rehabilitation is concerned, however, "what works" remains an open question. As Martinson[2] clearly pointed out, it is hard to determine how effective such programs were, because of the inadequacies of data and research, the variety of programs that were examined, and the different extents to which they were administered. Similarly, it could be argued that programs designed to reduce inequality and create greater opportunities were never sufficiently supported to produce tangible results.

Giving up on such alternatives to crime control out of hand is a matter of political and economic expediency rather than a reasoned approach to the problem. "Solutions" offered by politicians may help to alleviate some of the public's frustration (and will certainly garner votes), but thus far such policies have not demonstrably reduced crime. In fact, the situation has worsened, as courts receive more cases than they might reasonably be expected to handle, and prisons and jails overflow with inmates. We may feel safe in knowing that some criminals are behind bars, but given the horrible conditions of state prisons, we should be less comfortable knowing that these same inmates will eventually be released into society. In many states, prison conditions have become so hellish that courts have condemned them as inhumane. Our zealousness in giving criminals "what they deserve" has increased the U.S. prison population by almost sixty percent in the last ten years without a comparable increase in space to house them. The message from a beleaguered criminal justice system seems clear: there is but a limited capacity to punish.

Where have our policies gone wrong? Why can't we punish effectively and provide greater public safety through sound crime-control policies? Part of the answer lies with the notion that our legal system was never designed to take on the entire task of social control. This seems most true today, as the increased use of criminal punishment has been revived as the "solution" to the crime problem. The internal contradiction in such a policy lies in the fact that the same policy makers who endeavor to apprehend, convict, and lock away criminals claim that "less government" and "lowered public spending and taxes" are necessary for a better society. More importantly, however, the level of resources needed to realize this is so great, especially given large government spending deficits, as to render such an ideology problematic. Prisons are extraordinarily expensive propositions, and, according to many judges, more are needed to decently house the current prison population, even without additional inmates in the future.

Most experts today would agree that the criminal justice system does little, if anything, to "reform" criminals. The original goal of penal institutions in this country, which was the reformation of the criminal, has not been met in practice. This does not mean that such an ideal is impossible to achieve, but only that past attempts and methods have not succeeded. We have witnessed displacement of this original penological goal in favor of other goals, including retribution ("just deserts"), incapacitation (mere detention), and deterrence (curtailing crime through the fear of punishment).

The retributive justification of punishment is based on the notion of "just deserts." Most legal theorists argue that this rationale for punishment is necessary, at least to some degree, as it is the only one that contains the elements of justice and reciprocity in sanctioning criminals.[3] A recent study completed by a group of experts concluded that retribution should be the major purpose of punishment for similar reasons. They concluded that it was the strongest rationale, given the paucity of evidence on the effectiveness of other purposes of punishments.[4] While it is hard to argue with the idea that some kind of reciprocity is required in the meting out of criminal punishment, it is harder to specify the exact measure needed, as well as the form that it should take. This question may be interesting to social scientists, but is decided upon by legislators. The larger question necessarily arises as to the "justness" of retribution in what might be considered an unjust society.[5] That is, if all individuals are endowed with the same life chances, there is little ambiguity in what might be considered as fair or just; when they are not, the terms become more problematic.

Incapacitation refers to the mere restraining effects of imprisonment. Simple logic tells us that while incarcerated an individual cannot be out in the streets committing crimes. As a sole rationale for punishment, incapacitation is a dangerous doctrine in a free society. Relatively minor violations by "habitual offenders" could result in confinement for rather lengthy periods of time in order to prevent crime. Such practice would not only be extremely expensive, but would quickly exacerbate common notions of fairness and justice. While certainly effective for those confined, it is highly impractical and unjust as a major rationale for punishment.

Finally, there is the doctrine of criminal deterrence. This notion is tied to the utilitarian thinking of the classical school of criminology, most notably the writings of Bentham and Beccaria.[6] While there are many different forms of this concept,[7] two stand out in the scientific literature. First, there is "specific" or "individual" deterrence, which refers to the preventive effect that punishment has on an individual who is punished. The idea is that once a person has experienced the unpleasantness of punishment he or she will not want to engage in illegal behavior again. Studies of criminal recidivism have led most researchers to conclude that the chances of effecting specific deterrence are rather low. The second major type of deterrence is "general" deterrence, which refers to the effects of punishment on those not punished. Here it is the "example" of punishment that produces conformity in the general population. Over the past decade, criminologists have concentrated most heavily on testing the notion of general deterrence.

Originally, the concept of deterrence was tied to a larger reform movement in eighteenth- and nineteenth-century Europe, which advocated a more humane system of punishment based on the notion of "social good." It was posited that the certainty, the celerity, and, to a lesser extent, the severity of punishment would produce a "change of heart" in would-be criminals and thus prevent criminal activity. Punishment was seen as inherently evil and could not be justified, according to utilitarian doctrine, unless it could be demonstrated that more good than evil would result from its administration. Unlike retribution, the doctrine of criminal deterrence is "forward looking" and pragmatic in nature; the major function of punishment is seen as crime control. When certain, swift, and severe punishments are administered, the costs of committing crime are increased, which should lead to a subsequent reduction in criminal behavior. The doctrine has considerable merit in that it (1) provides a rationale for punishment that directly addresses the problem of crime control, and (2) states the conditions that must be met for punishment to act as an effective deterrent to crime.

What theorists and policy makers have failed to realize is that while deterrence may make good sense theoretically, it is much more problematic when applied to the realities of crime and criminal justice. While others have highlighted social and psychological processes and conditions as the major factors in the generation of crime (for example, social structural strain, subcultures that provide different normative and reward structures, the expressive rather than instrumental nature of many violent crimes, and rationalizations that serve to redefine the nature of the criminal act), and have either ignored or downplayed the importance of punishment, it is posited here that, even if assumptions about deterrence are absolutely correct, deterrence is largely doomed to failure as an effective means of crime control in practice. The argument assumes the following about the relationship between crime and punishment:

1. Crime is more a function of diverse social-psychological and social-structural phenomena than it is of legal sanctions.

2. Crime levels affect criminal justice practices just as much if not more than such practices affect levels of crime.

3. Punishment is most likely to be effective in deterring crime when it is needed the least—where crime rates are already low.

These assumptions are well in keeping with what Pound saw as "inherent difficulties of criminal justice," as well as with other major notions in criminology and the sociology of law.[8] The first assumption, that crime is more a function of extralegal factors than of punishment, can hardly be questioned, even by research that finds some evidence of deterrent effects. Such research has never found more than a minor amount of variance in crime rate that is presumably accounted for by criminal sanctioning. More importantly, however, sociologists and criminologists have established a wide and varied research literature that suggests from any number of (and sometimes even competing) perspectives that social-psychological, group, organizational, and societal (i.e., social-structural) factors generate both reported and actual levels of crime. Thus, the use of punishment to control crime is already limited; crime is more likely to be "controlled" by social phenomena outside the boundaries of the criminal justice system.

The second assumption, that crime levels affect criminal justice practices just as much if not more than such practices affect crime, is suggested in recent work by this author on "system capacity,"[9] as well as by others on "resource saturation,"[10] "system overload,"[11] and other similar phenomena having to do with the legal system's capacity to effect punishment.[12] Until quite recently, research findings of negative relationships between crime rates and certainty of punishment were almost exclusively interpreted as supportive of a deterrent effect. However, it is just as likely that such negative relationships are due to the system's relatively fixed capacity to deal with short-term increases in criminal activities. Increased work loads in criminal justice agencies require flexibility on the part of these organizations, with less certainty, severity, and celerity of punishment a likely result. Thus, the overloading of the criminal justice system might also produce negative relationships between crime and punishment. The greater the incidence of crime and the heavier the criminal justice caseloads, the lower the chances of punishment. This does not question deterrence in theory, but points to how deterrence may be largely mitigated in practice.

The third assumption is related to the second, but has different implications regarding deterrence as a viable means of achieving substantial crime control. It is in precisely those circumstances where deterrence might be most needed (conditions of high incidence of crime) that the criminal justice system is least able to effect it. This is the case for two main reasons. First, if criminal justice resources are relatively fixed at any given time, then environmentally induced increases in crime rates should translate into heavier criminal justice caseloads and a lowered capacity for generating and administering punishment. That is, low crime rates allow the legal system to be more punitive; where crime rates are high, the legal system cannot produce the conditions necessary for deterrence to operate effectively. A second related point concerns the population to which deterrence is mainly directed, the so-called crime-prone subgroups in society, which are disproportionately comprised of the poor. The bulk of criminal justice resources and processing activity is geared toward the sanctioning of common crimes, which are committed mostly by those in the lower class. Yet, the value of punishment is inherently lower for this group than for those with higher economic status, who necessarily have more to lose by engaging in crime. This is the case even assuming that deterrence doctrine is absolutely correct in theory. Those who have little, if anything, to lose by committing crime require relatively stronger negative messages from the criminal justice system in order to be deterred. Thus, even if the criminal justice system has the capacity to affect deterrence through legal sanctions, such effects will be differentially distributed in the population. The slightest deprivation for a person who has everything may incur a great deal of pain and discomfort; the same sanction for one who is already severely deprived may be meaningless.

While the analysis above may appear obvious to some, it has important implications for theory, research, and policy concerning deterrence and crime control. First, it suggests that attempts to deter what is perceived as increased criminal activity will be frustrated by the limited sanctioning capacity of the criminal justice system. As crime increases, the system may become more bogged down with heavy caseloads, reducing the probability of certain, swift, and severe punishments. Moreover, if criminological theories are correct in positing that inequality in the population accounts for a good deal of what is considered "serious crime,"[13] the likelihood of deterring such crime is placed in double jeopardy. Inequality would affect crime rates, which overburden legal machinery, and depress the value of punishment for those the system aspires to deter the most—the lower class. As crime and inequality mount, it becomes more difficult for the criminal justice system to deter violators.

The possibility of controlling crime through increased punishment concerns important theoretical as well as policy issues. Moreover, the prospect of achieving deterrence in an unjust society deserves closer scrutiny. This book focuses on these issues through an examination of the criminal justice system's capacity to generate and administer criminal punishment. The chapters that follow will discuss issues related to the study of deterrence as a means of crime control, review studies of criminal deterrence, present and elaborate on the system capacity model of criminal justice, and present an empirical analysis that documents and explores the capacity phenomenon. The final chapter will discuss the implications of the study for theory and research on crime and punishment as well as for social policies aimed at crime control.

II. The Deterrence Question

Within the past fifteen years there has been a major effort by social scientists to refine our knowledge about the doctrine of criminal deterrence.[1] Researchers have thus far compiled weak, yet supportive, evidence consistent with the deterrence hypothesis—a negative relation between crime and legal sanctions. It seems clear that under limited conditions the threat of punishment may be effective in preventing certain undesirable activities.[2] It also seems reasonable to assume that at least the threat of legal punishment is present, even if only in a symbolic sense, and may influence portions of the population.[3] If the threat of punishment was eliminated altogether, an increase in criminal activity would likely result. However, the types of legal sanctioning, population subgroups, and criminal activities needed to demonstrate the deterrence phenomenon have not yet been determined.

Deterrence research and theorizing have progressed rapidly in the past decade. The works of Andenaes,[4] Zimring and Hawkins,[5] and Gibbs,[6] among others, have increased our understanding of the ways in which legal threats may affect behavior. In addition, the study of "perceived sanctions," including the works of Waldo and Chiricos,[7] Henshel and Silverman,[8] Erickson, Gibbs, and Jensen,[9] and Grasmick and Bryjak,[10] has broadened the scope of research to include subjective awareness of punishment levels. These works also point to the complexity of the deterrence phenomenon—namely, the variety of circumstances and conditions that may influence the efficacy of legal threats to serve as inhibitors to criminal behavior.

These advances notwithstanding, research on deterrence may cloud the social reality of crime and punishment. By largely ignoring official labeling activities, including the ways in which defendants are prosecuted and convicted and the ways sanctioning activities themselves may be influenced by social processes existing both within and

9

outside of the legal system, the analysis of crime and punishment remains incomplete. The present study is an attempt to begin filling this theoretical void. Deterrence (even assuming that the doctrine on which it is based is absolutely correct) can only be realized to the degree to which the legal system has the capacity to detect, apprehend, and sanction violators. If one assumes that criminal punishments are determined simply by public will and legislative actions, then one might also reasonably assume that our society can effectively deter potential violators by increasing punishment levels. It is maintained here that criminal punishments are not manipulated simply by legislative actions, or the will of official actors, but that legal sanctions are the products of social and organizational forces.

The study of sanctioning activities in criminal courts can help provide important answers to questions about the rather positive findings of many ecological studies on the relationship between crime and punishment. Most analyses of crime and punishment are not very concerned with the ability of courts to generate and administer legal sanctions. That is, the capacity to punish is treated as a given or assumed condition in many studies, significant primarily as a possible deterrent to crime. Crime and punishment are inexorably linked phenomena and cannot be adequately examined apart from one another. The question of how punishment practices are affected by rates of crime has not received adequate attention. Yet, the examination of this relationship is necessary in order to evaluate the likelihood of deterrence in practice. An analysis which focuses on sanctioning activity in courts will help to identify the conditions under which criminal sanctions are likely to produce deterrent effects.

It may be that actual levels of criminal sanctioning have very little to do with deterrent or general preventive effects[11] as compared to perceived levels of punishment. Furthermore, extremely low levels of sanctioning by the criminal justice system would appear to encourage lawbreaking, if assumptions about deterrence are correct.[12] Those who are processed through the system, as well as their associates, would have more accurate information on criminal justice activities than those having no contact at all with the system. Their perceptions would likely be more precise and realistic than those of the ordinary population, who, according to Miller et al.,[13] tend to overestimate actual penalties. It is precisely this "criminal subgroup" that society would like to deter most of all. It is ironic that the criminal justice system may succeed in deterring, or, to use a better term, "preventing," certain behaviors in the general population while it may be less able to do so for "criminal subgroups" in society.

Even if sanctions were sufficiently strong to serve as general deterrents, the law would have to be perceived as carrying legitimate authority before punishment might have this deterrent effect. That is, those subjected to the law would have to hold it in respect before being restrained by it. This has been discussed in some detail by Johannes Andenaes[14] in his work on the concept of "general prevention."

There is a tendency in current research on the effects of legal sanctions to confuse, or treat as equivalent, the concepts of deterrence and general prevention. It is certainly true that the two are related, but there are also important differences, which highlight various purposes of the criminal law and its enforcement. According to Andenaes, the term "general prevention" is much more encompassing of the effects of legal sanctions on behavior than is "deterrence," or what he refers to as "mere deterrence." Mere deterrence has as its major notion the conveyance of a legal threat that will cause a change of heart in potential violators of the law. This is the same notion posited by the classical school of criminology—that the outweighing of pleasure by pain will prevent criminality. Economists have today changed these two latter terms to costs and benefits, claiming that less lawbreaking will occur where the costs are greater than the expected benefits to be gained through crime.[15] Although there are no exact formulas for calculating costs and benefits for individual crimes, it is generally assumed that some criminals are rational and will employ techniques for calculating whether to commit a particular crime. The main point, however, is that general deterrence, or, as Andenaes has described, "mere deterrence," has at its core the notion of calculation, the threat of punishment, and fear.

Andenaes refers to general prevention as "the ability of criminal law and its enforcement to make citizens law-abiding."[16] This includes not only deterrence (fear of punishment) but two other main components. The first is that the law may have moralizing effects that can produce both conscious and unconscious inhibitions to lawbreaking. Indeed, the cornerstone for any system of justice is that it achieve a general respect for the law among members of society. The legal system is but one institution among many—the family, education, religion, public and private groups and organizations—that affect the socialization process whereby individuals learn those social rules necessary for society to exist and survive. One of these norms for survival entails a respect for the law. Thus, besides simply scaring or threatening the populace into compliance, criminal punishment may also help serve as a moralizing and educative agent.

Another aspect of general prevention is that the enforcement of criminal law may act to create habitual law-abiding conduct.[17] We may come to see a particular behavior as "bad" or view it as "wrong" because the legal system views it that way. Punishment might attract our attention to particular undesirable behaviors and thus stimulate us to conform to society's concept of acceptable behavior. In this sense, criminal sanctioning acts as an "eye-opener," making us aware that certain behaviors are to be avoided.

The distinction between general prevention and "mere deterrence" is important for understanding how the legal system may affect behavior. A policy focused on deterrence and increased levels of punishment ignores the other ways in which the legal system could induce conformity. Fear of certain, swift, and severe punishment may seem like the strongest route for preventing crime, but fear alone may not induce conformity, nor may it be the most socially desirable way to create it.

It is dubious that most people are kept law-abiding most of the time through fear or calculations of costs and benefits. As Stone notes:

> When we look at the total social strategies that are available for keeping human beings in line, we see that the law is only part of, a complement of, more pervasive forces. What prevents most of us from committing murder is not based upon the threat of what the law will do, but mechanisms—guilt, shame, anxiety, conscience, superego—internalized within us through the forces of family, school, church, and peer group. By virtue of these processes a certain amount of potential antisocial activity is repressed or sublimated before it is even thought of. And a certain amount, though emergent into consciousness, can be stayed by moral argument ("Don't you see, you ought not to do that?") The law is only a last resort.[18]

Andenaes might amend this statement to say that the legal threat is only a last resort, but the point is made that there are a range of social control mechanisms available, punishment being only one. Fear and threat, components of deterrence, may, under certain circumstances, be unnecessary for general prevention to operate. General prevention is a broader concept than "mere deterrence," and, by losing sight of this fact, policy makers may unnecessarily rely on only the fear-producing aspect of punishment to formulate crime control policies.

III. Studies of General Deterrence

The doctrine of criminal deterrence provides one of the basic rationales for the use of punishment in modern society. It first appeared in the classic writings of Bentham and Beccaria and has had major influence on thought about criminal law and criminal justice policy ever since. Systematic empirical research on this subject has grown within the past ten years.

Andenaes, a leading theorist of general prevention and deterrence, noted that not much systematic sociological work existed on general prevention prior to 1970.

> While general prevention has occupied and still occupies a central position in the philosophy of criminal law, in penal legislation and in the sentencing policies of the courts, it is almost totally neglected in criminology and sociology. It is a deplorable fact that practically no research is being carried out on the subject. In both current criminological debates and in the literature of criminology, statements about general prevention are often dogmatic and emotional.[1]

The situation has changed greatly since Andenaes's assessment. A number of social scientists have been attempting to examine the validity of general deterrence.[2] Most deterrence researchers claim to have found evidence indicating that certainty and severity of punishment (certainty playing a greater role than severity) are instrumental in deterring criminal behavior.

Ecological studies of deterrence examine the effects of legal sanctions on rates of serious crimes in the population. This perspective aims at ascertaining the "general effects" of penal threats on those in the population who have not been incarcerated, as opposed to the "special effects" of penal sanctions on those who have been punished.[3] The following discussion is limited primarily to studies by sociologists in the area of general deterrence.

14

Sociologists have recently reshaped thinking and research on criminal deterrence; this "movement" began in the late 1960s. Preceding work tended to downplay the effects of formal sanctions, including the death penalty, in producing conformity.[4] The studies that began in the late 1960s are important because their somewhat positive findings resulted in a growth in deterrence research in the 1970s.[5]

Gibbs[6] published the first important sociological study on the general deterrent effect of imprisonment. The research was important not only because of its new data findings, but because it brought new attention to the study of crime and punishment. Considering only the crime of homicide, and using the state as the unit of analysis, Gibbs found that states with high levels of certainty and severity of punishment also have low crime rates, a finding that appeared to support deterrence theory. These results sparked new interest in the deterrence problem among sociologists.

Employing Uniform Crime Reports and National Prisoner Statistics as data sources, Gibbs introduced operational definitions of certainty and severity of punishment. The index of certainty of punishment consisted of the number of state prison admissions for homicide in 1960 divided by the mean number of homicides known to police for 1959–60. The index of severity of punishment was "the median number of months served on a homicide sentence by all persons in prison on December 31, 1960." Gibbs is cautious about inferring causal effects. He notes: " . . . all that can be said of the findings is that they question the common assertion that no evidence exists of the relationship between legal reactions to crime and the crime rate."[7]

Schwartz[8] published a study of the deterrent effect of severity of statutory punishment at about the same time as did Gibbs. Using Pennsylvania data on rape and attempted rape, Schwartz looked at variations in these offenses in the city of Philadelphia before and after statutory penalties were increased in 1966. He concludes:

> Philadelphia found no relief from forcible and attempted rape either during the excitement leading up to the imposition of stronger penalties for these offenses or after the imposition itself. This holds true with respect to both the frequency and intensity of these crimes. We are therefore bound to conclude that Pennsylvania's new deterrent strategy against rape was a failure as far as Philadelphia is concerned.[9]

Schwartz did not employ the same data or indexes as did Gibbs, so the results of the studies are not directly comparable. However,

Schwartz's results support the contention that changes in statutory penalties alone may have little effect on crime rate, which is in contrast to the pro-deterrent implications of Gibbs's research.

Gray and Martin[10] reanalyzed the data used by Gibbs by employing multiple correlation and regression techniques. Unlike Gibbs, they treated the data in interval form, preserving the original information which they contain. Using a simple linear regression model to measure the effects of certainty and severity of punishment on homicide rate, these researchers found that severity is more important than certainty in predicting homicide rate. The association, however, was extremely low. With no control variables included in the model, severity explained 13.5 percent of the variation in homicide rate, while certainty explained only 7.9 percent.

Gray and Martin noticed, however, that the lower the homicide rate, the less the association with certainty and severity of punishment—an observation which suggests a nonlinear relation. Using a curvilinear model, they found the same patterns as in the linear one, with even higher correlation ratios. They concluded that the curvilinear model is preferable to the linear one, in that it explains the difference in the effects of severity and certainty of punishment on the variation in homicide rate, and it makes more sensible predictions—the linear model predicted negative homicide rates, a logical impossibility.

Thus, the study by Gray and Martin reinforces the notion that punishment deters crime. The investigators differed with Gibbs, however, on the importance of severity of punishment. They found that severity may be of greater importance than Gibbs had originally claimed. Like Gibbs, they were somewhat cautious in their conclusion; they made no claims establishing causality. They note:

> Our model suggests that halving either certainty or severity of punishment will tend to double the crime rate, and vice versa; halving both will quadruple the crime rate, and doubling both will cut the crime rate to one-fourth its previous value—provided causality holds, a matter which is not testable with these data.[11]

The entire argument of Gray and Martin hinges on the assumption of causality among the variables. In addition, as the quotation above indicates, they are quite comfortable with the idea that punishment rates are easily manipulated by criminal justice authorities.

Bean and Cushing[12] also used regression analysis to reanalyze Gibbs's data. They replicated the finding of Gray and Martin, in that severity may be of greater importance than Gibbs had claimed. They introduced region of the United States (north and south) as an additional explanatory variable and found that it accounted for 62 percent of the variation in homicide rate, while "severity and certainty of punishment account for an additional 7.3 percent, an amount seemingly small but statistically significant."[13] It remains to be seen whether or not other influences would lessen the "explanatory power" of punishment even further.

Citing Wolfgang,[14] the investigators attributed the relation between region and homicide rate to the higher proportion of blacks in the south. They then proceeded to substitute proportion black for region as a control variable and found that the proportion of the variance explained by the punishment variables decreased from 7.3 percent to 5.2 percent. Again, it remains to be seen whether controlling for other possible causal factors would lessen the explanatory power of punishment to the point where it might become entirely negligible in explaining homicide rate, a possibility which the investigators do not mention.

Bean and Cushing conclude on a more optimistic note:

> After controlling for the substantial influence of proportion black as an etiological factor, the variable measuring legal reactions to crime retained its association with criminal homicide rate in a direction consistent with the deterrence hypothesis.[15]

If anything, the study shows how little influence certainty and severity of incarceration may have on homicide rate when only one etiological factor is controlled. If there is indeed a deterrent effect, it is likely to be a minor one in comparison with other phenomena related to reported crime.

Using indexes similar to those employed by Gibbs, Tittle[16] examined the effects of punishment on seven major felonies and a category of "total felonies." Tittle realized that defects exist in the data but assumed, as others before have, that the discrepancies do not vary widely from state to state.

Tittle, as did Gibbs, ranked the states according to their index scores, assigning an ordinal score to each state. He found consistent negative associations for certainty, but he also found that all crimes except homicide were positively related to severity. Unlike Gibbs, and Gray and Martin, Tittle found little evidence for an additive effect of certainty and severity of punishment.[17]

Tittle also controlled for the following variables: urbanization, educational composition, age composition, sex composition, and level of "modernism." He reported that all controls except urbanization had no effect on the relation between punishment and crime. In low urbanized states, the relation between certainty of punishment and total offenses was strongest, $-.36$, while in highly urbanized states the relation was only $-.16$. Tittle is aware that this does not necessarily indicate that punishment has a deterrent effect. He concludes that:

> It is reasonably clear that punishment does have some relationship to the amount of crime that becomes known to the police. This may be interpreted in several ways. It may be taken as evidence that the possibility of legal punishment has a deterrent effect. An alternative possibility is that low crime rates produce greater certainty of punishment.[18]

Tittle seems to favor the former interpretation, however. He states further:

> The data considered here do not permit full understanding of these phenomena, but the findings are sufficiently impressive to suggest that sociologists at least take the idea of deterrence seriously. It seems imperative that adequate explanation of societal patterns of conformity-deviance will require attention to official reaction to deviance.[19]

Tittle's analysis is very similar to those of Gibbs and Gray and Martin, in that he demonstrates that a relationship between crime and punishment may exist. Without serious attention toward the directionality of the relation, however, Tittle's conclusion as to the deterrent effect of certainty of punishment seems premature.

Following Tittle's study, Chiricos and Waldo[20] (using lagged correlations) attempted to measure changes in crime rates following changes in certainty and severity of punishment. Using the same data sources employed by Gibbs and Tittle, Chiricos and Waldo found low to moderate associations between certainty of punishment and six major felonies, for three different time periods. For severity, however, they found mostly weak positive associations. In contrast with Gibbs, Tittle, and Gray and Martin, they found no consistent support for the notion that severity of punishment deters homicides, or any other major felony.

Their analysis of percentage change in certainty and severity of punishment and rates of crime shows little support for the deterrence hypothesis. The relations between percentage change in certainty of punishment and crime rate "are both inconsistent in direction and low in magnitude."[21] They conclude:

> In brief, these data provide no support for the hypothesis that increased certainty of punishment will be followed by decreased levels of crime, or that decreased levels of certainty will be followed by increased crime.[22]

The same inconsistent and weak relations were found for percent change in severity and crime rate.

Chiricos and Waldo explain the inconsistencies in their results, and earlier, more supportive findings of deterrence, as possibly stemming from a statistical bias that arises from similar terms in the ratios that are correlated—certainty of punishment and crime rate.[23] Specifically, they claim that the similar term "crimes known to police," which is present in both the denominator of the certainty index and the numerator of crime rate, spuriously induces negative relations between certainty of punishment and crime rate. They argue further that Tittle's test for spuriousness is inadequate, and after recomputing the test themselves, they claim that "Tittle's findings for specific offenses probably do not exceed what could be 'automatically and spuriously produced' by the similarity of terms in his certainty and deviance indices."[24] They also point out that available aggregate data are not reliable enough for research on deterrence. Chiricos and Waldo suggest that future research should not be based on these data and that perhaps studies that examine individual cases would be more productive.

Logan[25] replied to the skepticism voiced by Chiricos and Waldo, pointing out that they had (1) used statistically unreliable measures of change (cf. Bohrnstedt, 1969), (2) chosen arbitrary points in time for measuring change, and (3) reached findings similar to Tittle's using the lagged correlation technique, even though their results were weaker. In addition, Logan claimed the simulation tests used by Tittle and Chiricos and Waldo are inadequate for assessing spuriousness in the ratio correlations because such tests assume that the terms in the ratios (imprisonments, crimes, and population) are unrelated to each other—when, in fact, they are all positively related. Logan maintained that part correlation is the most satisfactory method for testing spuriousness due to a so-called mathematical "artifactual effect" (as one measure increases, the other will tend to decrease). In part correlations, one variable is related to a second from which the effects of a third variable have been removed. Using this technique, Logan correlated crime rate with certainty of punishment after removing the effects of the common term crime from the certainty index. He found that relations between certainty of punishment and crime rate weakened somewhat but were still consistently negative. He concluded that these relations are not due to a mathematical artifact.

Logan points out, however, that the "excess" negative relation found by zero-order correlation is not necessarily spurious. Whether it is or isn't spurious depends on whether the relation between certainty of punishment and crime rate is considered to be a purely mathematical one or a causal association. If it is assumed to be a matter of mathematical artifact, then part correlation correctly assesses the relation. If the relation is considered to be causal, however, the excess produced by zero-order correlation may not be spurious (at least not by an artifactual effect). Regarding the possibility of causality, Logan states:

> It may be that the number of crimes places a strain on the legal system, which may lower certainty, or the level of certainty may negatively affect (by deterrence) the absolute number of crimes as well as the crime rate. Or perhaps some variable, like inefficiency and backlog in the courts, is positively related to the number of crimes and negatively related to certainty of imprisonment.[26]

Logan's research, perhaps more so than other early studies, points to the necessity of ascertaining the responses by police, agencies, courts, and prisons to serious crimes, as well as the effects that these institutions may or may not have on subsequent rates of crime. This crucial issue, which is related to criminal justice capacity, deals directly with the question of deterrence in practice and the actual sanctioning patterns of criminal justice agencies. Without adequate resources to deal with work loads, the activities of criminal justice agencies might undermine deterrence doctrine in that penalties would not be "swift, certain, or severe."

In conclusion, Logan points out that the problem of spuriousness due to indexical artifact should probably not have been raised in this context.[27] He cites statistical studies that show that when the ratios being correlated are theoretically meaningful as ratios, the problem of spuriousness does not arise.

Thus, according to Logan, the findings of Chiricos and Waldo do not, as the authors maintain, question previous research on deterrence. In a study published after his critique of Chiricos and Waldo, Logan[28] refined and extended the analyses of previous sociological studies of criminal deterrence. Using the same indexes, but treating the data on an interval scale, Logan examined the relation between punishment and crime through the use of regression techniques. After examining scatterplots of the data, he concluded that the data best fit a curvilinear model of punishment and crime; that is, the data form a downward curve that is steep at low levels of certainty and flatter at higher levels of certainty. Correlations of certainty and rates of crimes using both raw scores (the linear model) and log transformations (the curvilinear model) show that the curvilinear model produces slightly stronger associations for some crimes only. For severity of punishment, Logan found consistently low negative relations only at low levels of certainty, which suggests an interactive effect between certainty and severity of punishment.

Unlike previous researchers, Logan attempted to examine empirically the possibility that there is an effect of the number of crimes on certainty of punishment; that is, crimes may make demands on the legal system that could lower certainty. Part correlations were employed to ascertain this effect. Logan admits that this approach may be inadequate for this test, but the results showed that when the effects of number of crimes known to police were removed from the measure of certainty, the relationships between certainty and crime rates remained consistently negative. This result is questionable, however, since Logan removed the effects of crimes that were measured later in time than those used to construct the certainty of punishment index. It is also likely that the associations are inflated, since no control variables were introduced.

While not claiming to have shown a causal relation between punishment and crime, Logan states:

> ... the data have clearly shown an association between crime and punishment that is strong enough to warrant not only further research on deterrence but perhaps a general reexamination of some of the old rationalistic and utilitarian images of criminal behavior that criminologists may have too hastily abandoned.[29]

Encouraging as this may sound, Logan's analysis shows only that a relation between crime and punishment may exist, and hence he has not gone far beyond the findings of previous studies. Control factors need to be examined, and the directionality of the relation must still be ascertained before deterrence theory can be supported.

A U.S. Department of Justice study completed by Kobrin et al.[30] examines the possibility of deterrence at different levels of the criminal justice system in California. Using counties as units of analysis, and various measures of certainty and severity of punishment for the period 1968 to 1970, the study concludes that: (1) higher sanction levels are associated with lower rates of reported crime; (2) social (demographic) factors appear to have greater influence on crime rates than does the operation of the criminal justice system; and (3) the greatest potential contributions to crime control from the criminal justice system are found for sanctions generated at the police and sentencing stages of processing. This study is noteworthy for its attempt to differentiate among legal threats produced at different levels of the criminal justice system. The authors are careful to note that the potential effects of certainty and severity of punishment are likely to be minimal compared to the effects of social factors in the generation of crime. In this sense, the study represents an advance over previous research. However, it does not seriously entertain the possibility that crime and punishment are reciprocally related phenomena. Rather, the study was formulated with the assumption that criminal sanctioning patterns can be easily manipulated by authorities and statutory law.

Another study, by Tittle and Rowe,[31] is worth mentioning although it does not deal with penal sanctions. The research examines another legal sanction, certainty of arrest, as well as different units of analysis, cities and counties in Florida. The investigators found evidence for the notion that certainty of arrest must reach a "critical level" before it becomes associated with decreasing crime rates.

Scatterplots of the variables show that certainty of arrest must reach a 30 percent level before becoming associated with crime rate. On this basis, Tittle and Rowe conclude:

> The findings in this study suggest that certainty of punishment is an important influence on the degree of conformity that can be expected in a political unit, but that this influence does not show noticeable results until certainty has reached at least moderate levels.[32]

The introduction of seven demographic control factors does not alter this conclusion. The scatterplot for cities can be interpreted in a different light, however. It seems that the "critical level" of certainty of arrest is reached by only 29 out of 178 areas. The researchers do not ask why such a small proportion of cities in Florida reach the level needed to "deter" crime (if such a level exists at all). An alternative interpretation could be that low levels of crime allow for higher rates of certainty of arrest. It should also be noted that findings from this study are not directly comparable to those of previous deterrence studies since it deals with certainty of arrest rather than imprisonment.

CONCLUSION

General deterrence is essentially a phenomenon that reflects individual behavior (the weighing of costs and benefits and subsequent action). Research on this topic has been limited largely to the study of aggregate data on punishment and crime, however, due to the absence of individual data on criminal activities, perceptions of sanctions, and availability of alternatives to crime.[33] More recent studies have shifted to the study of deterrence using data on perceptions rather than objective levels of punishment. The foregoing review has treated early sociological attempts to explore the deterrence question through analyses of what statisticians call "observational data." Studies employing experimental and quasi-experimental research designs are not addressed in detail here. These latter studies have as a major shortcoming the inapplicability of results to actual settings of crime and criminal justice. The controlled conditions of experiments, by definition, do not approach the reality of the structure of crime and punishment in society. Also, studies using perceptual dimensions of punishment with noncriminal subgroups may not approach an understanding of the phenomenon with real criminals.[34] What these studies can tell us is that under special circumstances sanctions may deter. It is quite questionable whether these findings can be generalized to "crime-prone subgroups" in society. Such studies generally ignore the legal, social, and organizational realities of the generation and administration of criminal punishments by formal institutions of social control.

The economics literature on deterrence has also grown in recent years. Economists have tried to tackle the problem of reciprocity in the relation between crime and punishment. Statistical models employing simultaneous equations have been used in an attempt to disentangle the mutual effects of punishment and crime. Ehrlich's[35] work is among the most prominent in the economics literature. Because of what are known as "identification restrictions" in simultaneous equation techniques, however, Ehrlich's results on the deterrent efficacy of incarceration are difficult to assess.

A recent National Academy of Sciences report[36] notes two major obstacles in interpreting Ehrlich's and other economists' results on the general deterrent effect of incarceration. First, the effects of incapacitation are not controlled, thereby confounding the estimated effect of deterrence with effects of incapacitation. Second, and more important, the identification restrictions that must be employed in estimating simultaneous effects are generally not reasonable theoretically. This is true for all such studies which estimate simultaneous effects, not just Ehrlich's. The report notes:

> To obtain identification, Ehrlich's model assumes that demographic composition, urbanization, and economic conditions affect the imprisonment risk or police expenditures but do not affect crime rates. However, the strong interconnections among the many socio-economic and demographic correlates of the crime rate make it difficult to determine which among them do or do not have causal association with crime. Furthermore, it is simply not plausible to assume that none of the variables used by Ehrlich for identification causally affects crime while also assuming that each does influence either the probability of imprisonment, or police expenditures per capita, or both.[37]

The report concludes that the identification problem will continue to confound econometric research on deterrence until plausible identification restrictions can be found.[38] The report states further that due to basic sources of error introduced through identification restrictions, no definitive conclusions can be drawn from studies assuming simultaneous relationships.

> Assuming that there is a simultaneous relationship between crime rates and imprisonment sanctions, the Panel concludes that, because the potential sources of error in the estimates of the deterrent effect of these sanctions are so basic and the results sufficiently divergent, no sound, empirically based conclusions can be drawn about the existence of the effect, and certainly not about its magnitude.[39]

Thus, even when employing a highly sophisticated methodology to study deterrence, research still falls short in identifying "deterrent effects."

These studies are no doubt a response to the "failure" of modern criminology to incorporate the idea that legal sanctions may, under certain circumstances, reduce deviant behavior. Modern writers emphasize the notions of socialization into subcultures, failures of conventional socialization, psychodynamic problems, pressures generated by social contexts, and the reactions of others to the behavior in question.[40] While some deterrence researchers claim that social scientists have prematurely dismissed the concept of criminal deterrence, they do not adequately address the possibility that crime rates may affect sanctioning activities in the criminal justice system *more than* punishments may affect levels of crime.

Although deterrence researchers claim to have found evidence that penal sanctions reduce crime, they have only demonstrated that a negative relationship exists. This ecological association does not necessarily imply that punishment reduces crime. Do penal threats lessen crime rates by instilling fear in potential criminals, or does crime, affected by etiological factors, overburden existing criminal justice machinery and thus lower its capacity to generate and administer sanctions?

Although very little is presently known about factors that influence criminal punishment levels, certain trends in punishment are clear. Suspended sentencing, parole, and probation have come to replace imprisonment as major forms of punishment. This trend could indicate that penal practice has become much less reliant than formerly upon the logic of deterrence as a basis for operation. The widespread use of plea bargaining in criminal cases is another indication that statutory penalties are being lessened in practice, a condition that may indicate the general inability or unwillingness of legal institutions to apply certain and severe sanctions to suspected criminals.

In view of these considerations, it is reasonable to ask whether courts and prisons are capable of generating sufficiently frequent and sufficiently strong sanctions to deter potential criminals. Roscoe Pound[41] noted not too long ago that the messages communicated by the criminal law are probably too indirect and vague to have much effect as social control and deterrence. He saw this as an "inherent difficulty in criminal justice." Existing institutions appear now as they did then, overburdened by the work of processing violators. Further increases in the volume of crime may lead to further reductions in the certainty and severity of punishment. Deterrence researchers may thus continue to find negative correlations between crime and punishment; these correlations may even become stronger. It would be incorrect to attribute such findings to the deterrent effects of punishment. Yet deterrence research has supported the notion that sanctions deter crime on the basis of precisely such results.

As noted earlier, some investigators are aware of this basic problem. They claim that it is insoluble, however, because it is not possible to measure the effects of crime on punishment. For example, Tittle has written:

> High rates of crime could result in overcrowded prison facilities, thus inducing judicial personnel to make greater use of probation and suspended sentences. This would lead to a reduction in certainty of punishment as conceptualized here. Unfortunately judicial statistics are not adequate to test this alternative.[42]

Besides overcrowded prison facilities, high rates of crime could result in overcrowding of courts. It is possible to assess the plausibility of this alternative explanation by changing the time order of the variables.[43]

One of the major unexamined assumptions in the doctrine of deterrence is that the criminal justice system is capable of generating sanctions with sufficient strength and certainty to instill in potential violators a fear of punishment. It is no doubt true that people sometimes refrain from committing criminal acts for fear of possible negative legal consequences. It is also surely true that "decisions" depend on what most people *believe* will happen, rather than on *objective information* about what actually does happen.[44]

The question that remains unanswered (and largely unasked) is whether the criminal justice system can actually achieve general deterrence through its sanctioning activities. As present and past circumstances indicate, it seems likely that increasing rates of crime have limited the capacity of formal institutions of social control to legally punish criminals. The notion that levels of punishment can be raised in order to deter crime needs to be reconsidered.

IV. Reconsidering Crime and Punishment

Although there are rational-legal rules of criminal procedure and formal goals of punishment, legal authorities may use considerable discretion in the pursuit of these goals and in the application of the rules. This aspect of law permits informal arrangements to arise, including plea bargaining and other patterns of cooperation in criminal processing. Within such a system of interaction, which stresses norms of cooperation over legal norms of conflict, it would appear plausible that penological considerations, including that of deterrence, may become secondary to administrative and personal goals of participants. In addition, offices are not formally structured for cooperation. Rather, the organization of agencies is based on the norm of conflict, as an adversary system. The "demise" of the American adversary system has been noted by researchers who cite the informal, cooperative agreements that arise due to administrative necessity.[1] The extent to which this is true and the factors inducing such changes at a macrosociological level are generally not identified, aside from caseload and personal interests of individual actors. Does workload pressure influence the type and degree of sanctioning, including final sentence? Do rates of crime, arrest, and other demographic characteristics influence the sanctioning process? These important questions constitute the obverse of the deterrence question and, when examined, will further understanding of the relationship between crime and punishment.

In searching for deterrent effects, a formal-legal goal of punishment, researchers have tended to neglect the importance of the labeling process that occurs between arrest and final sentencing. While the formal goals of the criminal justice system may still be held by some actors in the system, by portions of the population, and by some

researchers as determining punishment and processing activities, this
may not be the case in practice. As crime rates have risen, there has
been no accompanying rise in the relatively severe punishment of
incarceration.[2] Furthermore, the certainty of punishment has declined in the recent past,[3] possibly indicating that the state's criminal
justice resources have been saturated.

The principal question now appearing is not how punishment practices influence rates of criminal activities, but how the organization of
criminal justice processing responds to caseload pressures that are
brought to bear upon it.[4] The transformation of the ideal adversary
system of justice to one characterized by some degree of cooperation
among actors demonstrates that "justice" does not necessarily conform to the rational goal model expressed by the traditional legal view
or to the statutory law itself. The adversary ideal, usually seen in
"spectacular" and highly publicized cases, is nowhere near a true representation of the criminal justice process today and, indeed, creates a
misleading picture that can only reinforce current practices. However, the quick adjudication of cases as characterized by such terms as
"assembly-line justice"[5] may also present a somewhat distorted picture
of criminal processing—one in which there is no adversariness.

Offices within the criminal court interact in the sanctioning process
primarily through informal arrangements, which arise, at least in
part, by administrative necessity.[6] While this has been a focus of research, the overall sanctioning patterns of the system resulting from
this process, and their possible relationships with external environmental factors and the structure of criminal justice agencies, have not
been examined within a single framework, and, as a result, we have
only incomplete knowledge of the generation and administration of
penalties. Rates of sentencing can be seen as representing the final
sanctions resulting from social and legal interactions.

The "Goals" of Criminal Justice

In current practice, agencies of criminal justice largely circumvent the
statutory law in the processing of cases. It is clear that individual
authorities have their own goals and needs—there is no "goal" or
"goals" of criminal justice in practice but only formal goals in the
strictly legal-traditional sense.[7] This helps bring to light the essentially
nonbureaucratic nature of criminal justice activities. There is no strict

hierarchy of authority in the Weberian sense of bureaucracy, but only a loose organization of separate offices, each with a certain degree of legal authority and each operating somewhat autonomously.

The replacement of formal organizational goals of criminal justice by a system of cooperative and mutually beneficial exchanges may be due, in part, to what Blumberg identifies as the "crush" of large caseloads and "systemic strains placed upon actors."[8]

> In order to meet production norms, a large variety of bureaucratically ordained shortcuts, deviations, and outright rule violations adopted as court practices exists.[9]

Blumberg's argument relies heavily on the caseload hypothesis of bureaucratic adjustment of processing activities. It appears that what Blumberg is saying is that in the absence of such pressing caseloads, a system of cooperative exchanges would not exist.

This is contrary, at least in part, to the findings of other observers of criminal courts. Mileski[10] finds that shortcuts and rapid processing tend to occur even when caseload pressure is less pronounced. Both Skolnick's and Cole's analyses[11] indicate that such patterns of cooperation not only may be due to workload pressures but may also be a consequence of long relationships and acquaintances among actors, as well as other administrative factors of which moving cases is only part. In a study of case disposition in Los Angeles, Mather[12] notes: "While caseload pressures are doubtlessly important, they may be overemphasized in the current literature." More recent studies by political scientists reached similar conclusions.[13]

COURT ORGANIZATION AND CRIMINAL SANCTIONS

Most deterrence studies have focused on the topic through a traditional model of the law, which takes for granted the formal decision-making process of the courts as outlined by statutory law. They examine how courts *ought to operate* if their activities conform to legal theory. Starting from such a perspective, such studies offer no "demystification" of the legal process that intervenes between the commission of a criminal act and final sentencing. Studied from a legal realist perspective, however, which emphasizes the "law in action," the legal process can be examined apart from its juristic appearance and in relation to wider society.

The traditional model of criminal justice coincides with that of "due process," or the ideal of the adversary system. In direct contrast to this ideal type stands the "crime-control model."[14] The former emphasizes the rights of the defendant and the elements of due process: the right to a jury trial, adherence to formal rules of procedure, the right to counsel and witnesses, cross-examination of prosecution witnesses, and the guarantee that no individual will act simultaneously as judge, prosecutor, and jury. The latter view, on the other hand, emphasizes an administrative-managerial approach to criminal processing, with a premium placed on "speed and finality."[15] Here, the presumption of guilt is necessary for the fast disposition of cases. In such an assembly-line atmosphere, the rights of the defendant are secondary to the organizational interests of the court, which evolve in part through the necessity of processing large inputs of violators.

Feeley[16] clarifies the organizational structure of the criminal justice system by contrasting what he terms the "rational-goal model" of the system with the functional systems approach. In so doing, he combines Weber's rational-legal model of organization with the goal model.[17] The major distinction between these two models is that "the rational model is concerned almost solely with means activities."[18] Feeley notes that it is possible to combine the two approaches, since, in the case of criminal justice, "means and goals merge."[19] He states:

> While on a highly abstract level, the goal—as opposed to the means—of the criminal justice system might be stated in terms of achieving justice, this goal has no clear empirical referent or context by itself. In the dominant tradition of the West at least, the goal, justice, usually acquires meaning in a normative, legal, and empirical context, only when operationalized in terms of procedure, i.e., means. Thus, particularly in the administration of justice, the means become the end, at least in terms of viewing "organizational effectiveness" and "formal goal activities."[20]

The important question which Feeley poses is how well the rational-goal model characterizes the *actual* organization of criminal justice. He argues that the emphasis on formal rules and decisions in studying the administration of criminal justice "tends to produce a *unidimensional* picture of the process by placing undue emphasis on one set of goals and rules without adequately considering other factors which are, perhaps, equally important in shaping the behavior of actors in the system."[21]

In contrast to the "rational-goal model," which Feeley creates for conceptual purposes, the "functional systems approach" views the organization of criminal justice as a set of activities based on "cooperation, exchange, and adaptation."[22] It emphasizes that the "rules" that are followed are not necessarily the procedural rules of law and that goals strived for need not be those that are espoused by those in the organization.

Thus, the idealized version of the criminal justice system as pursuing a single set of rational goals, such as "justice," or punishment for the sake of "deterrence," can be contrasted with a set of actors who pursue their own rational goals according to informal rules that arise to satisfy adaptive needs. Using such a perspective, it is possible to explore not only the adaptive activities of individuals in response to changes in the organizational environment, but the different processing and punishment outcomes that such changes may produce. Elements in the social environment of criminal courts, including workload pressures, which may result from disproportionately high rates of crime and arrest, are linked to final sanctioning outcomes through the effects that such factors have on administrative functioning. The distribution of resources among agencies of criminal justice in terms of their relative capacities for processing accused violators is likely to affect subsequent dispositions. This picture of criminal justice organization views the balance (or imbalance) between criminal justice components as dependent on environmental factors and their effects on the allocation of expenditures and personnel.[23] Factors that may influence the organizational capacities of criminal justice components, and hence the sanctioning process, may then be identified.

Besides the overall goal of "doing justice," which by itself cannot be examined,[24] the criminal court, through the production and application of punishments, has competing, and often conflicting, institutional goals. The "goals" of punishment may include rehabilitation of the offender, incapacitation, simple retribution, and general prevention, of which deterrence is a part. Administrative factors, such as moving cases, will also ultimately affect sanctioning outcomes and, in turn, potential deterrent effects.

CONCLUSION

The maintenance and functioning of the criminal justice system are based on norms of conflict as well as informal norms of cooperation. The combative stance of prosecutor and defense attorney was designed to ensure that due process be afforded those accused of criminal acts. In contrast to norms of conflict, however, norms of cooperation are likely to arise due to what Skolnick has termed the "administrative concerns" of actors in the system.[25] The defense attorney may want the best deal for his client but may also desire to dispose of the case as expeditiously as possible. The prosecutor has great demands placed upon his time by heavy caseloads and is responsible not only for moving cases within the system, but to the public at large. Thus, by what Skolnick portrays as "administrative convenience," the adversarial relationship is, to some degree, replaced by a system of mutually advantageous exchanges.

While it is well documented that formal organizational goals of the court may be replaced by immediate administrative concerns and goals of individual actors within the system, it is less clear how this transformation influences rates of final sanctioning and hence the potential effects of punishment. It seems reasonable to assume, however, that under such circumstances less punishment may result due to charge reduction at different stages of the process and promises of lenient sentencing during plea bargaining.

The statutory law sets limits on how criminal processing takes place. However, the law itself provides considerable discretion for authorities at different stages of processing. This allows the task of identifying violators and applying sanctions to adapt to changing conditions as needed. The statutory law does not, and seemingly cannot, dictate the process itself.

A changing social environment that produces increased rates of criminal activities, and hence a possibly greater input of violators into criminal justice agencies, taxes the existing social control resources of the state. In the vast majority of criminal cases, it is virtually impossible for the state to administer sanctions that are swift, certain, and severe, a nonpractice that stands in direct opposition to the major tenets of deterrence doctrine. This does not disprove deterrence, but rather indicates that its effects are likely to be greatly reduced in practice.

V. Framework for Analysis

It is posited here that rates of punishment depend on the sanctioning capacity of the criminal justice system—especially the courts. Sanctioning capacity can be considered a function of many factors: (1) the structure of the law, especially procedural law; (2) the formal and informal organizational relationships both within and among criminal justice agencies; (3) the resources given to the system's sanctioning arm, the courts (as both an absolute amount and relative to other agencies); (4) the social, political, and cultural milieu in which the court exists; and (5) other external environmental constraints, including the volume of cases to be processed. In an overall sense, sanctioning capacity can be viewed as the *willingness and ability of the criminal justice system to enforce laws and mete out punishment.* Whether or not punishment deters may be a moot question until we know more about the ecology of crime and punishment and the factors that affect the generation and administration of legal sanctions. Until we look more closely at the "crime rate system"[1] and at how punishments are generated, conclusions as to the deterrent effects of punishment may be premature. While it is difficult, if not impossible, to study the overall capacity to arrest, convict, and sanction violators, certain aspects of this concept allow for quantitative empirical analysis. The capacity of the judicial system to generate and administer sanctions depends in large part on the relation between resources and workload demands. Where resources are generous and demands light, sanctioning capacity is likely to be high. Sanctioning capacity is low where resources are scarce and demands heavy.

Workload demands are influenced directly by the number of cases a court is obligated to dispose of within a given time. Statutory law, and, more specifically, procedural law, which presumably functions to protect due process rights of defendants, also affects workload demands, but in a less measurable way. Court decisions have increased the rights of defendants and have thus limited the capacity of the state to prosecute and convict.[2]

It is hard to assess the effects such decisions have on court work loads. In a general sense, however, it would appear that the broadening of defendant rights has correspondingly increased the work of criminal courts in processing violators and of police in apprehending them.

Although judicial resources play an important role in determining sanctioning capacity, resources of other agencies in the criminal justice system also play important roles in the production of legal punishment. Most significantly, because of the pivotal role the prosecutor plays in bringing charges and negotiating cases, prosecuting resources will affect the capacity of courts to process violators. Perhaps of even greater importance, the proportion of police resources to prosecuting resources may account for the degree of caseload pressure in criminal courts. If police are funded heavily as compared to prosecutor's offices, disproportionate numbers of arrests may result in backlogged cases in the courts, necessitating earlier releases of suspects, more concessions during plea-bargaining sessions, and, hence, less certain and less severe punishments for those finally convicted.

Crime rates, influenced by environmental factors, may, in fact, lower sanctioning levels by taxing the limited resources of the criminal justice system. Recent work has given greater credence to this possibility.[3] Balbus[4] has shown a similar phenomenon in that the control apparatus of the state may temporarily expand in response to widespread turmoil but then must return to its stable level as soon as disorder subsides. Thus, research evidence suggests that criminal justice resources as a whole are generally fixed and unresponsive to short-term fluctuations in rates of crimes and arrests. Within the criminal justice system itself, however, certain resources are likely to be less fixed than others in the short term. The police, for example, receive resources from municipalities and are likely to receive additional funds when a rise in crime is perceived.[5] Also, the police receive almost twice the resources of courts and prisons combined.[6]

Political rhetoric concerning crime control focuses most heavily on increasing expenditures for police, potentially at the expense of other agencies of criminal justice and social programs aimed at alternative ways of reducing criminal activities.[7] The funding of the police force in relation to the courts may give rise to a "structured imbalance" between agencies and their capacities for sanctioning violators. Where this imbalance is more pronounced, less certain, less swift, and less severe sentences may result due to the disproportionately large caseloads the courts are likely to receive.

The effects of court caseloads on punishment are evident by the actions of prosecutors. The highly discretionary role of the prosecutor in charging defendants and in negotiating cases would appear to weigh heavily in considering this relationship. Prosecutors, to a great extent, determine the inputs the court must deal with and the outputs it produces in terms of sentencing. As Reiss[8] has noted: "By legal authority and by practice, prosecutors have the greatest discretion in the formally organized criminal justice network."

Prosecutors are, by and large, concerned with speed in processing large caseloads and with their image as measured by productivity (the number of convictions), rather than with considerations of deterrence. In addition, prosecutors who are faced with large caseloads must choose only the most favorable cases, that is, those where a plea of guilty can be obtained quickly and easily and those where there is "adequate" evidence of guilt. The fact that the capacity of the court to prosecute is limited is evident from the high attrition rates as cases move through the system. For example, Mather[9] reports that at pretrial screening of felony cases in Los Angeles, "prosecutors exercise considerable discretion at this point, filing felony complaints on only about one-half of the felony arrests."

Because prosecutors are elected to their positions, their "track records" (convicted defendants), which reflect how well they are protecting the public, strongly influence their future careers. They must produce conviction statistics that place their activities in the best possible light. This is likely to take precedence over other concerns of due process, social justice, and deterrence. Prosecutors strive for high rates of conviction, and correspondingly low rates of acquittal and dismissal, once cases are accepted. This is, in part, accomplished through the semiofficial practice of plea bargaining. In fact, it has been estimated that as much as 80 to 90 percent of criminal cases are disposed through plea bargaining.[10]

Prosecutors must try to bargain most cases in order to meet calendar requirements of the court and to manage the large caseload that confronts them. Thus, they must drop cases that are in some respect problematic, and negotiate pleas of guilty, which carry the promise of less punishment, for all cases that remain. Where caseload pressure is greatest, less formal sanctioning is likely to result.

The model of crime and punishment presented here is different from other such models by and large, which have been constructed from a concern with identifying deterrent effects of punishment. Rather, this model is derived from the assumption that legal sanctioning—the celerity, certainty, and severity of punishment—depends, to a considerable degree, on the organizational structure of the court and also on factors external to the criminal justice system. In addition to organizational resources and workload demands, the model includes two other key variables that may affect the sanctioning process: inequality and crime. As explained in more detail below, the model incorporates the idea that the amount of crime in a given jurisdiction may be a determinant of punishment,[11] and that inequality (i.e., the extent of differences in living conditions among the civilian population) may affect levels of both crime and punishment.

INEQUALITY, CRIME, AND PUNISHMENT

The relationship between social inequality and what is considered serious crime is widely recognized by social scientists as holding a key to the process of criminogenesis.[12] Income disparity, unemployment, poverty, racial segregation, and other components of social inequality all play a role in the production of crime. There is also evidence that official indicators of crime, or reported crime, may largely be a function of the activities of official agencies, namely police organizations, and of reporting patterns in the population.[13] Inequality is also likely to play a major role in the use of punishment, in terms of both quantity and type.[14] I shall attempt to join these two seemingly independent sets of relationships through an examination of their ecological linkages.

One critical theoretical connection is found in the proposition that the deterrent value of criminal sanctions depends upon conditions prevailing outside of the criminal justice system itself.[15] That is, rates of legal sanctioning may not be as important in and of themselves for assessing general deterrence as seeing these rates in light of, and indeed necessarily tied to, prevailing social and economic conditions.[16]

For example, when a large pool of surplus labor develops, the prison population can be expected to increase. Both are consequences of a slowed economy, and the miserable conditions of the poor are surpassed by those in the prisons. According to the notion of "less eligibility," punishment must establish a greater deprivation than that already suffered by the lowest free class.[17]

The most elementary concept of punishment is that it involves deprivation of valued states and social relationships. If utilitarian assumptions about general deterrent effects are correct, then as socially valued states and relationships increase in the population (i.e., as the standard of living is raised) less punishment or deprivation should be necessary to achieve a comparable degree of general deterrence. Because the *value* of punishment is necessarily greater during times of prosperity, fewer resources can be spent on punishment to achieve a similar level of deterrence. If this is the case, then there is a further contradiction tied to the use of punishment to control crime. The value of criminal punishment is highest when crime rates are likely to be low.

Christie[18] clarifies the notion of the deterrent value of criminal sanctions with his closely related idea concerning the penal value of punishment:

> In a community where the ordinary population enjoy increased leisure, imprisonment will be regarded as an increasing evil, its penal value will rise sharply, and therefore less of it can be used to compensate offenses committed.[19]

Besides offering an explanation of how penal values change and of how they are related to social conditions, Christie's analysis also sheds light on how equal punishments may have differing values for different social classes. The "ordinary population" to which Christie refers is unlikely to include the indigent and minorities, who are generally excluded from mainstream society's consumption patterns. Because of the lowered state of living conditions for these groups, the value of punishment is necessarily lower than in the "ordinary population." Thus, according to utilitarian doctrine, more punishment is necessary for offenders from these groups than is warranted for those from the middle or upper classes. Christie's notion of penal values may help to explain varying punishments for different classes within society, just as it may hold true generally for society as a whole.

Varying penal values may also explain inequality in the imposition of criminal labels and punishments. Contemporary research on sentencing has focused on the judiciary[20] and the defendant in terms of extralegal characteristics and the offense charged.[21] These studies generally ignore the concept of the penal value of sanctions, however, which is not directly measurable. Rather, it is embedded in the social fabric. Lower-class offenders already have less to lose by committing crime than those in higher social strata. The value of punishment is therefore necessarily less for the lower-class offender. Authorities may thus feel justified in meting out more severe and certain punishments to this group. On the other hand, less punishment is generally warranted for the relatively well-to-do. One recent example of this is evident in the case of Watergate. The Watergate defendants, after having been found guilty of what might easily be considered as rather serious crimes and abuse of the public trust, were rather leniently sentenced. In fact, there was even widespread skepticism as to if what had transpired could really be considered "crime." It appeared that "deprivation" and punishment for these individuals were imposed according to their high status. Perhaps brutal punishment was not "rational" or called for under such circumstances. On the other hand, for those with little to lose in the first place, punishment has less inherent force. Theoretically, a greater measure of it is necessary to further deprive the already deprived criminal.

Recent research on judicial attitudes toward sentencing white-collar offenders supports this view.[22] Judges are still grappling with the inherent paradox in making sentencing decisions where the defendant is a highly valued member of the community. If a severe sentence is imposed, the defendant's family will suffer, and so might the interests of the community; if the sentence is not harsh, the goal of deterrence and overall justice may not be served.

Thus far we have ignored the fact that most white-collar criminals are seen as committing "less dangerous" kinds of crimes.[23] Fewer white-collar criminals are likely to have long criminal records, which will also influence the sentences they receive. These last two points clearly help account for the meting out of fewer and less severe sanctions for white-collar crime. Yet, these explanations relate only to *rates* of sentencing of white-collar versus common criminals. The "penal value hypothesis" accounts for differences in sentencing for rather similar combinations of seriousness and prior record between both white-collar and common criminals, and, more importantly, seems congruent with the notion that judges are likely to be lenient with white-collar criminals.[24]

This discussion points to what could be considered as the class-structured nature of punishment in American society. It is already an established fact that most persons arrested, convicted, and sentenced to prison are from the lower social strata. They are least likely to be represented by private attorneys, most likely to be convicted of "serious" crimes, and most likely to be sentenced to imprisonment and death row.

As inequality in society mounts, the rate of crime is likely to increase.[25] At the same time, however, economically induced increases in inequality among portions of the population reduce the deterrent value of criminal sanctions for such groups. Rusche and Kirchheimer[26] document this through their examination of the relationship between penal practices and general economic conditions in European countries. They found that the presumed deterrent effect of punishment could only be maintained by keeping prison conditions more miserable than the situation of the lowest free class. This is necessary if punishment is to deprive the criminal. They also found that prisons became overcrowded with violators when there was a large pool of surplus labor. During such economic circumstances, crime rates increased, as did the number of capital crimes. The subsequent overcrowding of prisons served as a natural mechanism for keeping conditions of prisons below that of the lowest free class. Prison conditions thus reflected and magnified the brutality of life facing those at the bottom of the social ladder.

If no other factors were at work, therefore, changes in social conditions producing inequality would translate into higher crime rates and higher rates of punishment in terms of severity and certainty. This view neglects, however, the limited capacity of present-day institutions of criminal justice to administer sanctions. Imprisonment rates for the past few decades may have reached an equilibrium.[27] This means that while recorded crime rates have risen, punishment has leveled off. This is likely to indicate (1) the saturation of penal resources, and (2) possible changes in penal values.

As mentioned earlier, other likely determinants of sanctioning activities include criminal justice resources and court workload pressures. The effect of public spending on criminal justice agencies as a determinant of sanctioning may appear obvious. That actual patterns of criminal justice expenditures may create discrepancies among agencies within the legal system that could impact on the sanctioning process itself, however, is generally less appreciated. That is, if police resources are disproportionately large in comparison to judicial resources, criminal courts may fall increasingly behind in processing cases, necessitating earlier releases of detained defendants, increased dropping of charges, more plea bargaining, and less sanctioning. This is most likely to happen in urban areas where reported rates of serious crime are high.

If inequality grows in society, then rising crime rates are a likely consequence.[28] Growing public concern over safety may translate into the opposite of its intended effect by creating further imbalances in criminal justice funding. For example, greater funding of the police in relation to courts and prisons may result in overcrowded court and prison facilities thereby necessitating lowered levels of punishment. Here the concept of overload and its relation to the sanctioning process becomes important in understanding the ecology of crime and punishment. A high degree of workload pressure is brought to bear on criminal courts through the interaction of high crime rates and relatively low expenditures. The police, via arrest, create work inputs for courts and prisons. The combination of high reported crime and disproportionate spending on police relative to courts and prisons may be a major source of the seemingly ever-increasing workload pressures noted by observers of criminal courts.[29] The influence of caseload pressure on sanctioning practices, and the efficacy of legal punishments in achieving general deterrence given such practices, need to be explored.

Using Official Statistics on Crime and Sanctions

A major criticism of most quantitative studies on crime and punishment is that they take official statistics at face value, or as indicative of some individual underlying social phenomenon.[30] Official summary statistics are likely to reflect the totality of interactions of a number of underlying phenomena. For example, it is already well known that recorded rates of crime (crimes known to the police) seriously underestimate the extent of crime in society. This may appear to present no major problem when examining internal variation within a set of data,[31] but it may lead to erroneous conclusions for other reasons.

First, it is still unknown how crime rates may be influenced through the interaction of actual deviance and official attempts to record it. What crime statistics really reflect is a combination of legal recording capacity and actual crimes. The activities of local police departments, including such things as patrolling methods, data recording mechanisms, and interactions with different complainants, are likely to affect the types of deviance that are recorded.[32] In addition, the police concentrate their energies disproportionately on certain types of crime. A consequence of this is that many serious white-collar crimes are not represented in official statistics. Thus, official methods of crime control and data recording may influence known rates of criminality as much, if not more than, actual amounts of such behaviors. It may also be that people are reporting more incidents even though the actual number of incidents remains constant. This points to a basic inadequacy of such data, which is that they do not accurately portray the phenomenon of primary theoretical interest: actual levels of criminal behavior.

Secondly, aggregate data on crime within some geographic unit can only be used to show ecological relations with other phenomena. Official data reflect criminal justice production figures more than attributes of individuals. In particular, crimes known to the police, as reported by official agencies, reveal little about the criminal activities of groups of individuals in terms of their sex, age, and race. Conclusions about the behavior of individuals from such data are incorrect (the ecological fallacy), but inferences can be drawn concerning the unit of analysis used (state, county, census tract, etc.).

Using arrest statistics to approximate a better measure of criminal activity is of little help. They are even more likely to reflect the activities of police—especially their efficiency and methods of patrol—rather than the true extent of criminal activities. As Gilbert Geis notes:

> Arrest statistics reflect in myriad ways the procedures, paradoxes, and idiosyncracies involved in the business of law enforcement. For instance, an efficient police force will often become aware of a greater number of offenses and will arrest a larger number of persons than will a less efficient police organization. Summary statistical reports, taken at face value (which is the way such reports are almost always taken), imply that a better agency is less effective in reducing crime than a less capable agency, a curious juxtaposition of the facts of the situation.[33]

Besides this problem of taking such statistics at face value is the fact that they are also not fine enough to allow for a detailed understanding of what they are actually measuring. What these data really represent are total "production figures" of various criminal justice agencies. They reflect the *totality of activities* of legal authorities.

It is argued here that what is needed is a critical use of such figures rather than an abandonment of their use altogether. Certain assumptions will need to be made concerning their validity, but they can be used to theoretical advantage once their shortcomings are recognized. This points to what may be called the "unofficial use of official statistics." Many studies in criminal justice and criminology tend to neglect the official meanings and activities that go into the classification and generation of government data. Giving these data credibility, and especially scientific worth at their face value, is a problem that has been noted in the literature.[34] The many pitfalls inherent in official data can be at least partially reduced by giving criminal statistics a different meaning, namely, as production measures of criminal justice agencies (instead of traditional meanings intended by authorities). These statistics can then be more effectively used to describe "global" relationships among crime, the legal system, and society.

Global variables are useful for examining the *sum* of lower level social processes.[35] As they apply to the criminal justice system and deterrence, such variables may aid in uncovering unintended consequences of different and separate legal activities in the criminal justice system and their possible relationships with social structural characteristics. What the criminal justice system "produces" in terms of crime rates and legal sanctions can be linked to population characteristics through the analysis of global variables.

Statistics on court processing reflect the totality of interactive processes that occur during case disposition. Reasons for dropping charges, the background of the defendant, original charges, as well as other considerations, cannot be described from these data. Rather, official statistics reflect the totality of all interactions during case disposition. At the level of the jurisdiction, or criminal justice system, however, generalizations may be made from such data.

The preceding discussion points to the possibility of using official statistics as criminal justice production figures. Production figures of organizations are many times employed for purposes of legitimation, that is, for perpetuating certain myths concerning the organization's functions and activities, as well as for justifying increased allocations of resources. As Meyer and Rowan note:

> Ceremonial criteria of worth and ceremoniously derived production functions are useful to organizations with internal participants, stockholders, the public, and the state as with IRS or the SEC. They demonstrate socially the fitness of an organization.[36]

High rates of arrest and conviction justify the activities of legal authorities. Officials are aware that such figures put them in a good light—they are "dealing with criminals" and performing efficiently—and justify increased resources for their agencies.[37] Criminal justice statistics generally reflect this idea of "ceremonial criteria of worth." As a consequence, their theoretical use at face value for explaining and understanding questions of interest to researchers is extremely limited. Reformulating these data may provide more meaningful theoretical measures. Until more accurate data are made available, transforming existing data into "less official" indices may provide the only way of examining relations among crime, law, and society. This approach releases the research endeavor from examination of "ceremonial data," which are likely to cloud basic issues concerning criminal justice activities and relationships between these activities and wider society.

In the following examination of the ecological linkages among crime, legal sanctioning, and society, six major areas will be examined. These are: (1) rates of felony crimes reported to the police; (2) resources per capita, in terms of both personnel and expenditures for criminal justice agencies; (3) expenditure imbalance between agencies and the degree of caseload pressure in criminal courts; (4) felony court conviction rates and method of case disposition; (5) rates of punishment produced by criminal courts in terms of sentencing outcomes; and (6) demographic features of California counties. These factors will first be examined in terms of their median values for California counties over the period 1966–1974.[38] These measures will then be examined in terms of their relative rates of change over the same time period. Finally, the ecological associations among these variables will be examined through the use of correlational techniques.[39]

DATA

This study employs data on California counties for the time period

1966 to 1974. Although limited to a single state, the investigation
draws on what is considered to be one of the most extensive and
uniform bodies of criminal justice data in the United States. These
data are assembled and published yearly by the Bureau of Criminal
Statistics and Special Services of the California Department of Justice.
State law requires counties to report offense, disposition, and resource information according to definitions established by the
Bureau. Thus, jurisdictional differences in reporting are likely to be
smaller than in national data sources. Moreover, the possible confounding variation introduced by differences in criminal law is controlled, since California's 58 counties are governed by the same state
law. Besides offering finer units of analysis than states, counties also
represent the political units in which court sanctioning naturally occurs. That is, felony cases are adjudicated in county superior courts.
Finally, the broad scope of criminal justice data provided in the
Bureau's reports allows for the representation of crime, punishment,
and resource variables of interest in this study.[40]

Thus, county data from California seemed well suited for this research. For the time period examined, California was the largest state
in the country. It is similar to other large states (New York, Texas,
Illinois, and Pennsylvania) in terms of the diversity of its economy and
population. It is not unlikely that the findings of this research would
be generalizable to these states and possibly to others. Similar analyses
would be needed, however, for a more accurate assessment of this
probability.

Information on criminal justice resources (spending and personnel), arrests, crimes, convictions, and sentences was derived from reports issued by the Bureau of Criminal Statistics.[41] Other aggregate
data on demographic characteristics were derived from figures kept
at the California Bureau of Finance and from the *City and County
Databook* published by the Federal Bureau of the Census.

The years chosen for study were largely a function of the availability of such data. After meetings with officials at the Bureau of Criminal Statistics, it was clear that the nine-year period of 1966 through
1974 contained the only time series data that would be comparable
according to the data collecting procedures of the Bureau, and, at the
same time, provide the necessary information for measures of crime
and court sanctioning. Adequate prison data were not available from
this source, and time and resource restrictions in the study precluded

their collection. While such data are certainly important in assessing the system capacity model of crime and punishment, an adequate analysis can be performed concentrating on the sanctions produced at the court level. Data on prisons might be used in conjunction with that already collected in order to assess, in future studies, the relationship between prison overload and court sanctioning. The main task of this research is to report on the manifest relations among elements of social structure and criminal justice organization and function in courts to assess the likelihood of deterrence.

VI. Changes in Crime, Punishment, and Court Processing

RATES OF CRIME

Rates of reported serious crimes across California from 1966 through 1974 are shown in figure 1. The seven major index offenses included in the category of total felony crimes are homicide, rape, assault, robbery, burglary, theft, and auto theft. These felony crimes are further defined as personal crimes (homicide, rape, and assault) and property crimes (robbery, burglary, theft, and auto theft). Of the three crime rates measured, personal crimes show the highest percent increase for the nine-year period (167 percent). This is followed by the overall felony crime rate (105 percent) and the property crime rate (94 percent). It should also be noted that, on the average, reported serious property crimes outnumbered personal crimes about ten to one. This ratio would likely be decreased if unreported personal crimes, especially rapes and assaults, became known to authorities.

The total felony crime rate shows a little over a 100 percent increase, from 1.6 per 100 population in 1966 to 3.3 in 1974, or a doubling in the nine-year time frame examined. The medians, semi-interquartile ranges, first and third quartiles, and the number of counties on which these measures are taken are displayed in Appendix 1.

Figure 2 shows percentage changes of median rates of reported crimes in California counties. All three rates of crime show about a 70 percent increase between 1966 and 1971. A leveling off is observed between 1971 and 1972, especially for property crimes. Between 1972 and 1974, the last two years measured, the property crime rate resumed its upward trend at a rate similar to that previous to 1971. The average number of personal felony crimes, however, increased dra-

46

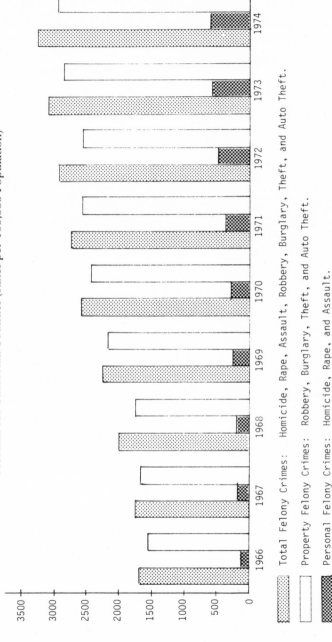

FIGURE 1 Rates of Reported Serious Crimes 1966–1974
Medians for California Counties (Rates per 100,000 Population)

Total Felony Crimes: Homicide, Rape, Assault, Robbery, Burglary, Theft, and Auto Theft.

Property Felony Crimes: Robbery, Burglary, Theft, and Auto Theft.

Personal Felony Crimes: Homicide, Rape, and Assault.

Source: Bureau of Criminal Statistics and Special Services, County Criminal Justice Profiles.

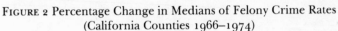

FIGURE 2 Percentage Change in Medians of Felony Crime Rates
(California Counties 1966–1974)

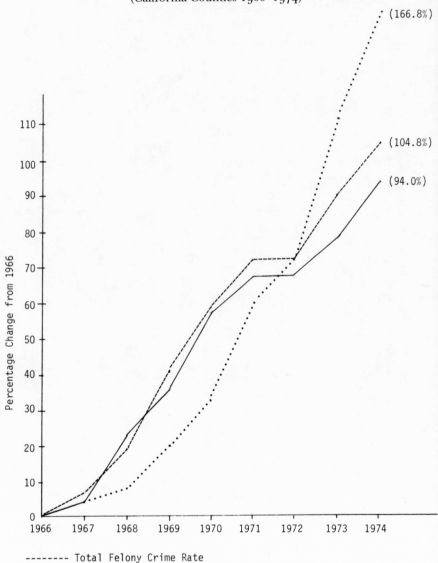

matically between 1972 and 1974. While the median reported personal crime rate for California counties increased by about 70 percent between 1966 and 1972, it shows an increase of 167 percent through 1974. Whether this reflects only an actual increase in such crimes is questionable, and a definitive answer to this sudden increase cannot be offered. It is possible, however, that increased public awareness and social support groups and services for personal crime reporting (e.g., rape hotlines), as well as better data recording mechanisms of official agencies, may have been at least partly responsible for this sudden jump in reported violent personal crimes.

Criminal Justice Expenditures

Figure 3 presents median levels of spending in dollars per capita for criminal justice agencies in California counties. The agencies included are police, prosecuting offices, and superior court. The data presented in figure 3 represent total expenditures for each agency. The prosecution category includes all prosecuting resources from both the superior and the lower courts. Superior court expenditures represent mainly judicial personnel costs, as well as ancillary personnel (clerks). These data were not available for 1966 or 1967, leaving seven years for study.

Figure 3 clearly shows the vast differences in average spending for police services as compared to court-related services. This difference remained almost constant for the seven years examined.

In 1968, median per capita police spending in California counties was $15.90, compared to $1.50 for prosecutorial services and $1.00 for superior court services. In 1974, these median per-capita figures were $30.60 for police, $3.40 for prosecution, and $1.50 for superior court. This represents an increase in medians over the seven-year period of 92.5 percent for police spending, 126.7 percent for prosecutorial services, and 50 percent for superior court (see Appendix 2). While prosecutorial services show the greatest percent increase in median spending, it should be noted that for all years examined, the ratio of median police spending to median prosecutorial spending was about ten to one.

Figure 4 shows the percentage increase in median criminal justice spending levels from 1968 to 1974. Police spending shows the great-

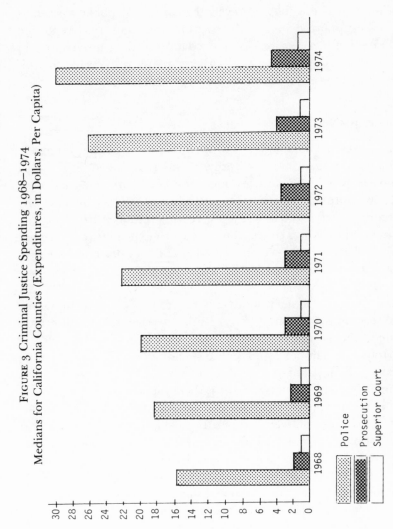

Figure 3 Criminal Justice Spending 1968–1974
Medians for California Counties (Expenditures, in Dollars, Per Capita)

Police

Prosecution

Superior Court

Source: Bureau of Criminal Statistics and Special Services, County Criminal Justice Profiles.

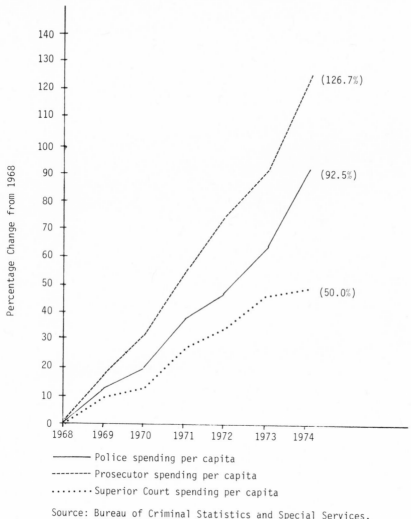

FIGURE 4 Percentage Change in Medians of Criminal Justice Spending
(California Counties 1968–1974)

Police spending per capita
Prosecutor spending per capita
Superior Court spending per capita

Source: Bureau of Criminal Statistics and Special Services,
County Criminal Justice Profiles.

est increase between 1973 and 1974, from about a 66 percent increase in 1973 (measured from 1968) to a 93 percent increase in 1974. Similarly, median prosecutorial spending shows an accelerated increase for the same period, from a 93 percent increase in 1973 to a 127 percent increase in 1974. Judicial expenditures show the slowest rate of increase, only 50 percent by 1974. The increase was fairly constant, except for a slight leveling off between 1969 and 1970.

Despite the accelerated growth of prosecutorial over police resources (figure 4), the data show about a ten to one ratio (police/prosecutor) between median expenditures over the seven years examined (figure 3). Even more pronounced is the difference in medians between police and judicial expenditures. In 1968, the ratio of median police expenditures to superior court resources was approximately sixteen to one. In 1974 this ratio increased to about twenty to one. This is important because discrepancies between criminal justice component resource levels are likely to impact on the processing of accused violators. Where this relative difference is greater, court caseloads may increase, which, in turn, could result in less certain and less severe punishments.

In conclusion, it should be noted that in 1974 all criminal justice expenditures (including corrections) accounted for 12.2 percent of total general expenditures in California. The nationwide figure was only 8.8 percent.[1] Thus, California spent proportionately more on its criminal justice agencies than most other states, or the country as a whole. In that same year, California spent about 52 percent of its total criminal justice budget on police, 28 percent on corrections, 12 percent for the judiciary, and 6 percent for legal services and prosecution. Nationally, these figures were 56 percent for police, 23 percent for corrections, 11 percent for the judiciary, and 6 percent for legal services and prosecution.[2] Comparatively, California spent 4 percent less of its criminal justice dollar on police and 5 percent more on corrections than the nation as a whole. These differences, however, appear to be insignificant. Overall, patterns of criminal justice spending in California in 1974 were quite similar to those of other states, although the percentage of total state expenditures allocated to criminal justice agencies was higher in California than in most other states, giving the state a larger criminal justice system relative to most other areas.

CRIMINAL JUSTICE PERSONNEL

Figure 5 displays median rates of criminal justice personnel per 100,000 population for the period 1968 through 1974. Personnel levels are shown for police, prosecution (data not available for 1968), and superior court. As was the case for expenditures, no data on corrections personnel are available from the Bureau of Criminal Statistics. Also, similar to the expenditure data, the personnel figures for prosecution represent both superior and lower court services.

Median levels of criminal justice personnel in California counties between 1968 and 1974 display a pattern similar to that of expenditures. The ratio of median police personnel to prosecutorial personnel per capita was approximately ten to one for the period examined. The ratio of median police to judicial personnel in superior court was between seventy and eighty to one. As found earlier for expenditures, the personnel data also reveal the large size of the police force relative to other criminal justice agencies.

All agency personnel levels measured experienced an increase over the time period examined. Median prosecutorial personnel (measured from 1969 to 1974) shows the largest increase, from 16 to 22 per 100,000 population—an increase of 37.5 percent. Median police personnel levels grew from 181 in 1968 to 227 per 100,000 population in 1974, an increase of 25.4 percent. For the same time period, median superior court personnel increased only 3.7 percent, from 2.7 to 2.8 per 100,000 population. The medians, semi-interquartile ranges, first and third quartiles, and number of counties on which these measures are based are shown in Appendix 3.

Figure 6 displays percent changes in median levels of criminal justice personnel per capita. Measured from 1969, prosecutorial personnel shows the greatest percent increase through 1974—37.5 percent. It shows an increase for every year measured, and a slightly lower rate of growth between 1970 and 1971 and between 1973 and 1974. The greatest increase is observed between 1971 and 1973. Police personnel experienced a rather steady rate of growth between 1968 and 1972, increased sharply in 1973, and resumed its previous growth rate in 1974. In contrast, superior court personnel was rather stable for the time period examined, showing a slight drop between 1968 and 1969, followed by a gradual rise until 1973 and a subsequent decline in 1974 to about its initial level in 1968.

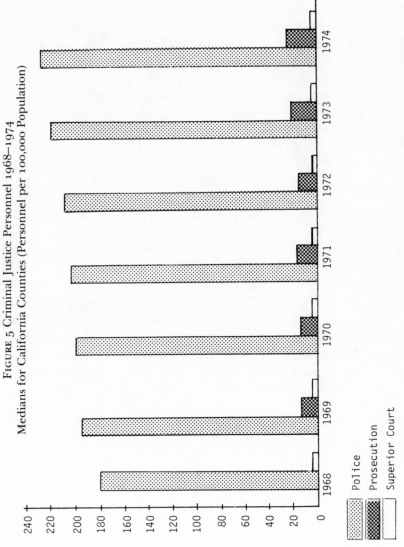

FIGURE 5 Criminal Justice Personnel 1968–1974
Medians for California Counties (Personnel per 100,000 Population)

Police

Prosecution

Superior Court

Source: Bureau of Criminal Statistics and Special Services, County Criminal Justice Profiles.

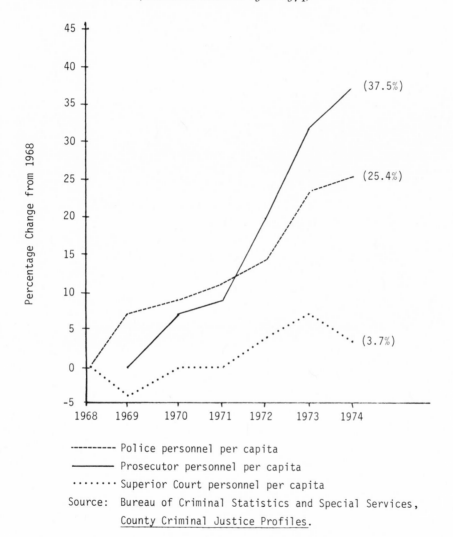

FIGURE 6 Percentage Change in Medians of Criminal Justice Personnel
(California Counties 1968–1974)

-------- Police personnel per capita
———— Prosecutor personnel per capita
········ Superior Court personnel per capita
Source: Bureau of Criminal Statistics and Special Services,
County Criminal Justice Profiles.

As might be expected, due to inflation and increased salaries, the percent increases in criminal justice capacity measured by personnel are not as great as those for expenditures. An increase in median prosecutorial expenditures of 127 percent translates into an increase of only 38 percent in prosecutorial personnel. Similarly, police expenditures increased about 93 percent while personnel showed only a 25 percent increase. A 50 percent rise in superior court expenditures produced only a 4 percent increase in personnel. Thus, while expenditure levels show large increases between 1968 and 1974, increases in personnel were low by comparison.

Means of Conviction

Figure 7 displays the median values of methods of conviction in superior courts for the period 1966 to 1973. Three means of conviction were available from the official summary statistics used in this study. They are (1) original plea of guilty, or "fast" guilty plea, (2) changed to guilty plea, or "slow" guilty plea, and (3) tried guilty. The tried guilty category includes trials by jury, court, and transcript. All three means of conviction are measured as a proportion of all convictions in the superior court, allowing a comparison of rates of processing across jurisdictions. In this form, they represent measures of adversariness at the court level, "original guilty pleas" showing the least adversarial proceeding, and "tried guilty" representing the most adversariness in disposing cases.

Before considering these rates of adversariness in felony courts, a comment on total convictions is needed. The conviction rate is measured as the proportion of convictions to court dispositions. In California counties, the median conviction rate shows little change over the eight-year period studied. In 1966, the median conviction rate in superior courts was .87, or 87 percent of all cases disposed, compared to .89 in 1973. Thus, on the average, about nine out of ten cases in superior courts resulted in conviction of the defendant. This does not imply, however, that the defendant was convicted of the offense originally charged. (This point will be discussed in the following section on "level of conviction.") The high average rate of conviction, almost 90 percent throughout the eight years examined, was likely due to initial case screening by the prosecutor. At this stage of processing, as much as 50 percent of all filed cases may be dropped.[3] The cases that remain

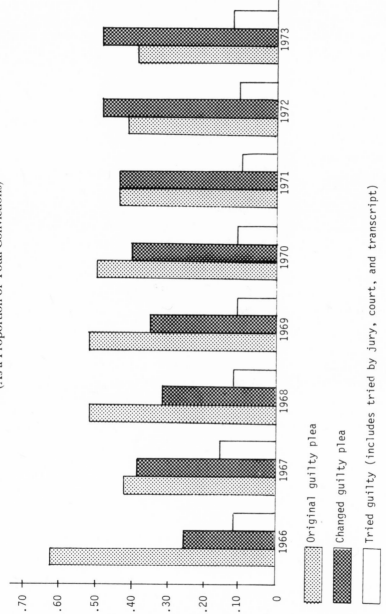

FIGURE 7 Superior Court Means of Conviction 1966–1973
Medians for California Counties
(As a Proportion of Total Convictions)

Original guilty plea

Changed guilty plea

Tried guilty (includes tried by jury, court, and transcript)

Source: Bureau of Criminal Statistics and Special Services, County Criminal Justice Profiles.

will be favorable for the prosecutor in that they will likely result in a conviction obtained by a plea of guilty. Serious offenses, and those for which the prosecutor feels "solid evidence" exists for conviction, are the most likely to be retained for processing. This surely contributes to the very high conviction rates found here and noted by others.[4]

Figure 7 shows that the vast majority of convictions were obtained through plea bargaining. For the time period measured, the median rate of all guilty pleas was between 85 and 90 percent of all convictions (original guilty plea and changed to guilty plea combined). On the average, trials accounted for about 11 percent of all convictions during the period 1966 to 1973. These findings are not surprising, given other results from research on criminal courts.[5] What is interesting, however, is the change in the dominant means of securing convictions. In 1966, on the average, over 60 percent of convictions were obtained by original ("fast") pleas of guilty, the least adversarial means of conviction. In the same year, changed ("slow") pleas of guilty, on the average, accounted for 27 percent of convictions in superior courts, while trials accounted for only 13 percent. In 1973, seven years later, this pattern was dramatically different. The dominant means of conviction in 1973 was the changed to guilty plea, which, on the average, accounted for 47 percent of convictions, while original pleas of guilty accounted for 39 percent.

Figure 7 displays the gradual climb in slow guilty pleas. In 1972 slow guilty pleas became the dominant mode of conviction in superior courts. Original pleas dropped from an average of 62 percent of all convictions in 1966 to only 39 percent in 1973. During the same time period, slow pleas rose from an average of 27 percent to 47 percent of all convictions. These figures, in addition to the semi-interquartile ranges, first and third quartiles, and number of counties, are presented in Appendix 4.

What this translates into in terms of percent changes is displayed in figure 8. In relation to total number of convictions, fast, or original, pleas of guilty, which indicate the least adversarial proceedings, declined by 37.1 percent between 1966 and 1973. A quick drop in this average is observed between 1966 and 1967, followed by a slight increase in 1967, a leveling off in 1968, and a gradual decline again through 1973. Slow, or changed, guilty pleas, show the sharpest increase in 1967, followed by a moderate decline in 1968, and a gradual rise which levels off in 1971–1972. The overall increase in "prolonged

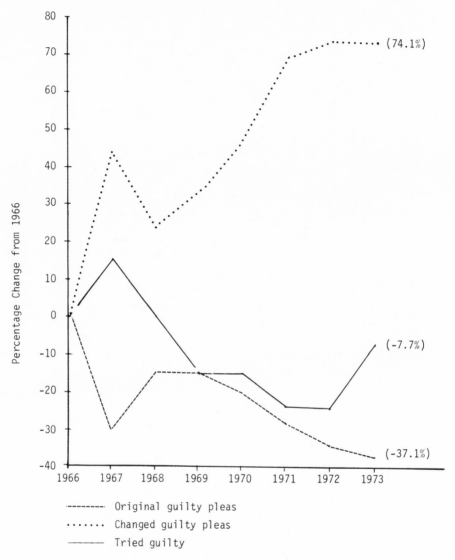

FIGURE 8 Percentage Change in Medians of Superior Court Means of Conviction
(California Counties 1966–1973)

------- Original guilty pleas
······ Changed guilty pleas
——— Tried guilty

Source: Bureau of Criminal Statistics and Special Services,
County Criminal Justice Profiles.

bargains" is 74.1 percent. The average rate of convictions obtained through trials shows an increase between 1966 and 1967, a decline through 1972, and a subsequent rise in 1973. This measure remained relatively constant, declining only 7.7 percent over the seven time periods examined.

These results can be interpreted as showing an overall increase in adversarial proceedings in superior courts. In 1966, fast pleas of guilty represented the dominant mode of conviction in felony courts. By 1973, this situation had changed significantly. Slow pleas of guilty, which are indicative of more conflict between the state and the accused, became the major source of conviction in California superior courts. Possible reasons for this change will be discussed in a later section dealing with correlates of adversariness.

LEVEL OF CONVICTION

Figure 9 displays the proportion of convictions resulting in a felony sentence. This percentage remained relatively constant for the period 1966 to 1973. There was a slight decline in the rate of felony sentencing between 1967 and 1969, and a gradual rise thereafter. The median level of felony sentencing in superior courts is 68 percent of all convictions in 1966 compared to 79 percent in 1973. This amounts to a 16.2 percent increase over the time period examined. The median level of misdemeanor sentencing is 32 percent of all convictions in 1966 and 21 percent in 1973, a decline of 34.4 percent (see figure 10).

It is important to note that the level of conviction is determined by the type of sentence imposed and not the charge.[6] That is, the figures cited above reflect the median rates of *type of sentence imposed* and not the *actual conviction* on specific charges. After conviction on felony charges, it is possible for judges to use their discretion in sentencing to set the conviction at the level of a misdemeanor.[7]

It is interesting to note that a steady decline in misdemeanor sentencing occurred after 1969, the year that Section 17 of the California Penal Code was amended (see figure 10). This change in law allowed certain lesser felonies to be processed as misdemeanors. This meant that "less serious" felonies (mostly drug, assault, and forgery cases) that would have been processed by the superior court were processed instead in lower criminal courts. It is estimated that approximately 6,000 defendants were shifted to municipal courts in 1970 under

FIGURE 9 Superior Court Level of Conviction 1966–1973
Medians for California Counties
(As a Percentage of Total Convictions)

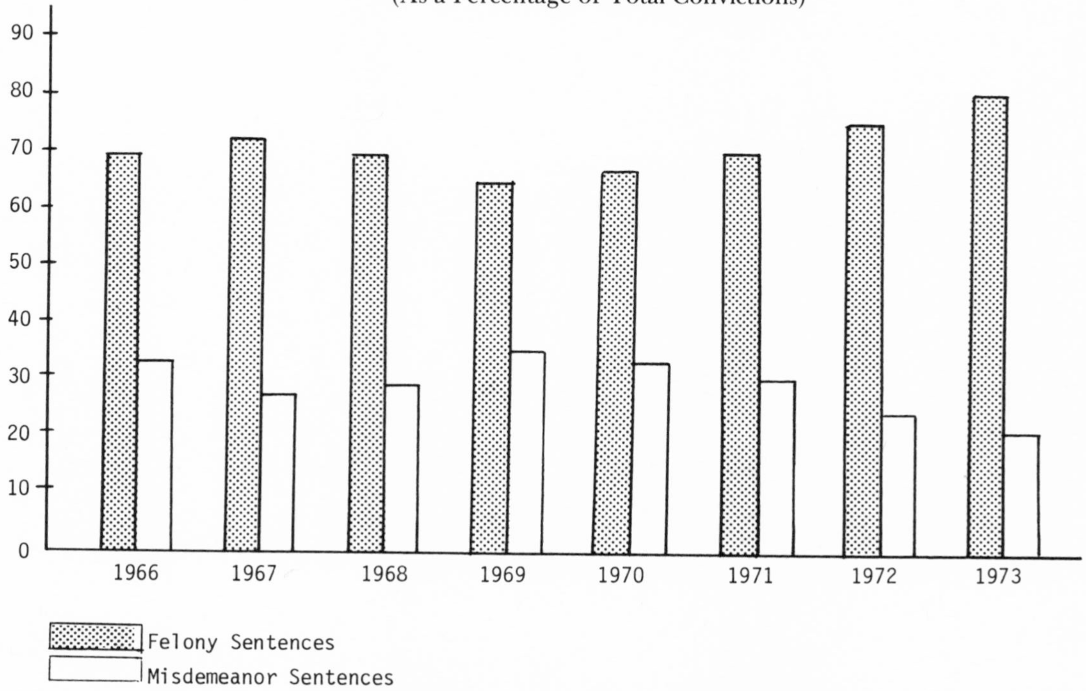

90
80
70
60
50
40
30
20
10
0
1966
1967
1968
1969
1970
1971
1972
1973
Felony Sentences
Misdemeanor Sentences

Source: Bureau of Criminal Statistics and Special Services, County Criminal Justice Profiles.

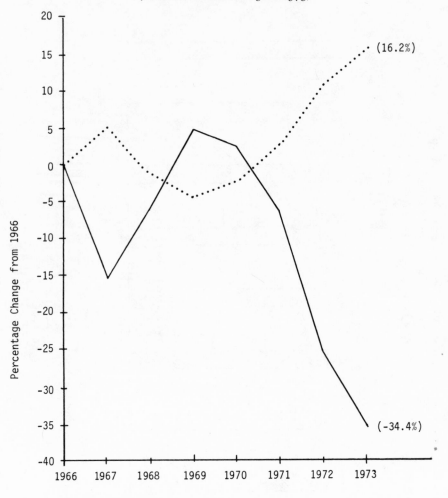

FIGURE 10 Percentage Change in Medians of Superior Court Level of Conviction
(California Counties 1966–1973)

•••••• Felony sentence rate

———— Misdemeanor sentence rate

Source: Bureau of Criminal Statistics and Special Services,
County Criminal Justice Profiles.

Section 17.[8] These cases, because of their less serious nature, would be more likely to be bargained down to misdemeanor convictions in superior courts. Without these cases in superior court, one would expect that the proportion of felony sentences would necessarily rise after 1969, which is exactly what is found in figure 9. Appendix 5 contains the medians, semi-interquartile ranges, first and third quartiles, and number of counties on which these figures for felony and misdemeanor sentencing rates are based.

Clearly, the data show that the majority of defendants in California superior courts are likely to be convicted through bargaining and to be sentenced at the felony level. This appears to indicate rather certain punishment for offenders. The actual sanctions imposed, however, are not evident from these findings.

It should also be noted at this point that not all criminals are apprehended, nor are the ones who are caught certain to have charges brought against them by a prosecutor. Mather[9] notes that in Los Angeles in 1970 only about one-half of all arrestees were processed through criminal courts. This attrition of violators at initial processing stages certainly reduces the likelihood of punishment. Thus, while conviction rates and felony sentencing are quite high (as shown by the data here), the proportion of alleged violators exposed to these sanctions is not. Furthermore, judges in California have great discretion in making sentencing decisions. A conviction at the felony level does not necessarily mean that the judge will incarcerate the defendant. The sentences imposed in superior courts are discussed in the following section.

SENTENCING

The median rates of superior court sentencing for the period 1966 to 1973 are presented in figure 11. The four categories of sentence considered here are prison, probation with jail, jail only, and straight probation. Other commitments, such as fine, California Youth Authority, and the like, are not shown. The median rate for the total of these "other commitments" is less than 15 percent of all convictions for any given year included in this study.

It is also important to note that the sentencing data say nothing about actual punishments carried out by the state. That is, the information reveals nothing about suspended sentences or length of time

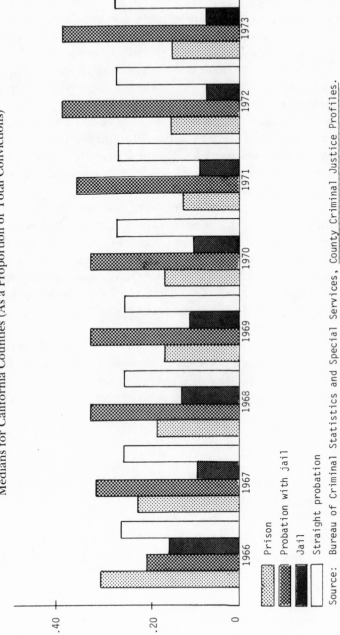

FIGURE 11 Superior Court Sentencing 1966–1973
Medians for California Counties (As a Proportion of Total Convictions)

Prison

Probation with jail

Jail

Straight probation

Source: Bureau of Criminal Statistics and Special Services, County Criminal Justice Profiles.

served in prisons and jails or on probation. Thus, the measures presented here represent only the potential types of sentences that may be served by those convicted.

Median rates of prison sentences in superior courts, measured as the proportion of prison sentences relative to all convictions, declined over the years studied (see figure 11). In 1966, prison was the most frequent sentence (29 percent), followed by straight probation (23 percent), probation with jail (20 percent), and jail only (15 percent). In 1973, this ranking changed markedly. On the average, probation with jail was the most frequent sentence meted out by superior courts (37 percent), followed by straight probation (26 percent), prison (15 percent), and jail only (8 percent). These measures show that while average rates of straight probation sentencing remained relatively constant over the time period examined, rates of prison sentences declined, as did jail only sentences. Probation with jail sentencing showed a marked increase in 1967, followed by only a slight rise thereafter. Rates of prison sentencing, the most severe sanction measured here, ranked third in frequency, behind probation with jail sentencing and straight probation, for all years studied except 1966. By 1973, an average of only 15 percent of defendants convicted in California superior courts were sentenced to prison. In terms of actually serving time in prison, this percentage is surely reduced by cases for which the sentence was suspended. Thus, only a small fraction of convicted defendants ever served a prison term. If one considers those who were not prosecuted or arrested, the certainty of serving time becomes even smaller. The data show that those convicted were most likely to serve time on probation, sometimes with jail. The medians, semi-interquartile ranges, first and third quartiles, and number of counties on which these statistics on sentencing rates are based are included in Appendix 6.

Figure 12 presents the relative rates of change for each sentencing category. Of all sentencing rates examined, probation with jail shows the highest percent increase between 1966 and 1973 (85 percent). Straight probation sentencing remained relatively constant, increasing only 13 percent over seven years. Median rates of both prison and jail sentencing show similarly large decreases over this same time period (-48.3 percent and -46.7 percent respectively). The largest changes in these measures occurred between 1966 and 1967 (see figure 12).

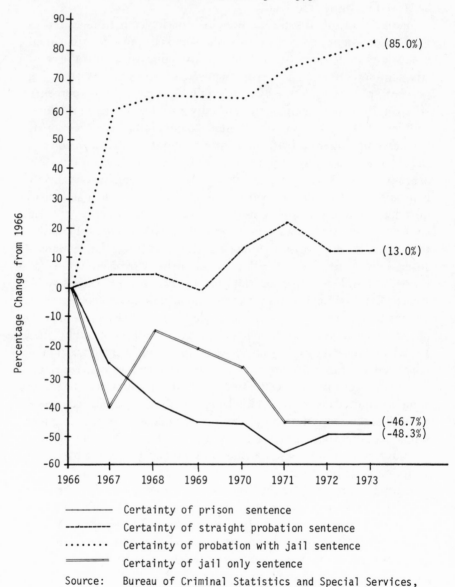

FIGURE 12 Percentage Change in Medians of Superior Court Sentencing
(California Counties 1966–1973)

—————— Certainty of prison sentence
--------- Certainty of straight probation sentence
.... Certainty of probation with jail sentence
═══════ Certainty of jail only sentence
Source: Bureau of Criminal Statistics and Special Services,
          County Criminal Justice Profiles.

The indisputable finding from these data is that the probability of receiving a severe sanction once convicted was extremely small. On the average, most defendants convicted in superior courts were sentenced to straight probation or probation with jail. It would appear that under such circumstances of limited severe sanctioning, the deterrent efficacy of punishment is likely to be minimal.

It should also be noted that changes in punishment rates correspond quite closely to changes in means of conviction (figure 8). The increase in probation with jail sentencing (85 percent) corresponds to the increase in the proportion of convictions obtained through slow guilty pleas (74 percent). Similarly, percent decreases in prison and jail sentencing (-48 percent and -47 percent respectively) follow the decline in original (fast) guilty pleas (-37 percent). This finding may point to the negative effect of slow pleas on severity of sanction. Fast pleas will normally entail less charge reduction and hence provide potentially higher maximum penalties for defendants. As this means of conviction decreases, less punishment may result.

POTENTIAL AND ACTUAL COURT CASELOAD

Potential caseloads for superior courts vary, depending on the environment in which the court is situated. Resource differences between police and prosecutorial components, for example, could affect actual caseloads in courts. The greater the police resources compared to prosecutorial resources, the greater the potential for heavy court caseloads. Another measure of potential caseload pressure is felony arrest rate. Influenced by the size of the police force, police efficiency, citizen complaints, and actual levels of criminal activities, felony arrests represent potential cases in superior courts. Where arrest levels are relatively high, courts may be under increased pressure to dispose of large numbers of cases.

A third measure of potential court caseload is dispositions per capita. The number of cases a court disposes of relative to the size of its jurisdiction reveals the activity of superior courts in relation to the size of their social environments. Courts that process more cases relative to population size could be considered to be "more active" within their jurisdictions. This measure represents the volume of court activity relative to population size more closely than it does actual caseload pressure. It allows for comparisons to be made among courts along a

single continuum of relative processing activity. Using this standard-
ized measure, which is different from volume measured simply by
number of cases, relationships among the degree of court activity, the
social environment, and actual court caseload can be examined.

The ratio of police expenditures to prosecutor expenditures remains relatively constant between 1968 and 1974, showing only a 6
percent decline.[10] The ratio of police to prosecutor spending ranges
from 9.67 to 1 in 1968 to 8.94 to 1 in 1970. For the remaining years it
is always at least 9 to 1. In contrast, the second measure of potential
pressure in court processing, felony arrest rate, shows a marked increase between 1966 and 1974—almost 160 percent. Dispositions per
capita, the third indicator of potential caseload, shows a moderate
increase of 45 percent between 1966 and 1973, from 1.63 to 2.36.

Of the three measures of potential caseload pressure, felony arrest
rate and dispositions per capita show the only significant increases for
the time period examined. The proportion of police expenditures to
prosecutor expenditures shows only a slight decline.

Court caseload is represented here as the ratio of superior court
dispositions to all prosecuting personnel within a particular jurisdiction. Data on superior court prosecuting resources only were not
available. However, it could reasonably be assumed that the proportion of superior court prosecuting resources to lower court prosecuting resources should not be dramatically different across jurisdictions. Finer data on prosecutorial resource levels are needed to test
this assumption. To the extent that this assumption is correct, the
ranking of superior court caseloads is well represented. But in absolute terms, the figures obtained do not reflect the actual number of
cases per prosecutorial personnel in superior courts.

Actual caseload pressure, which is measured here as the number of
dispositions in superior court per prosecutorial personnel, shows a
decline of 21 percent between 1969 and 1973. Thus, while average
arrest and disposition rates increased in California, caseloads declined. This seemingly paradoxical finding is likely explained by the
measure of caseload employed and the effects of a change in Section
17 of the Penal Code, which, as mentioned earlier, directed lesser
felonies to lower courts.

Regarding Section 17, which became effective in 1969, the implica-
tion for changing caseloads seems clear. The purpose of this change

in law was to reduce caseload at the superior court level by allowing lesser felonies ("wobblers") to be processed in lower courts. The decline in caseload between 1968 and 1973 may, in part, reflect the effect of this change in law.

In conclusion, it must be emphasized that a general increase in potential pressure over time, accompanied by a reduction in average actual caseload, does not necessarily mean that the two phenomena are inversely related or unrelated altogether.

SUMMARY

Thus far, the analysis has dealt only with average changes in the variables of interest to this study. Certain overall trends have been identified. The data show an overall increase in the rate of reported felony crimes of 105 percent between 1966 and 1974. Criminal justice resources, measured in terms of spending and personnel at the organizational levels of police, prosecutor, and superior court, show average increases between 1968 and 1974. Also noted is a change in the dominant means of conviction in felony courts between 1966 and 1973. While original (fast) guilty pleas were, on the average, the major means of conviction in 1966 (62 percent), in 1974 they constituted only 39 percent of all convictions. This indicates the slower processing of cases. Thus, it could be argued that the system showed greater adversariness over time. While convictions at the felony level increased over the time period examined, sentencing rates went down in superior courts in terms of the certainty of convicted defendants receiving relatively harsh punishments. Both jail and prison sentences decreased (47 percent and 48 percent respectively), while sentences carrying probation with jail were used 60 percent more than initially. Overall, there was an increase in potential caseload pressure measured by felony arrest rates and court dispositions per capita. In contrast, actual caseload pressure showed a slight decline (21 percent), which seems partly due to Section 17 of the Penal Code.

The question of how these measures of crime, resources, defendant processing, caseload, and punishment are interrelated is taken up in the following chapter. In addition, the relations among these variables and demographic characteristics of California counties are described.

VII. Relations among Crime, Punishment, and Society

RATES OF CRIME

Correlations between demographic characteristics of California counties and rates of felony crimes in 1970 are shown in table 1. A weak, yet statistically significant positive correlation is found between both reported personal crimes and property crimes and the degree to which the county is urban in character. The percentage of blacks living in the county shows the highest positive correlation with crime rate, followed by the percentage of males aged 25 to 29. The percentage black in the population is used here as an indicator of the degree of inequality in the population.[1] It is also noted that the percentage of young males in the population (19 years and under) is negatively associated with the felony crime rate.

Even stronger than the observed relationships between demographic characteristics and felony crime rates are the associations between police resources and crime (see table 1). The correlations between both police expenditures and police personnel per capita and felony crime rates vary between .88 (police personnel per capita and felony property crime rate) and .92 (police expenditures per capita and felony personal crime rate). While these associations are quite high, both the direction and sign of these relations are under debate.[2] It is important to note, however, that while felony crime rates are highly related to police resource levels, and moderately associated with superior court resources, there is no significant association with prosecutorial resources. In fact, the signs of the near zero correlations with prosecutorial personnel levels are negative. Thus, while police and court resources may be responsive to and influential toward rates of crime, the data show no interaction between rates of recorded crimes and prosecutorial resources. This finding may have serious

70

TABLE 1 Felony Crime Rates by Demographic Characteristics and Criminal
Justice Resources Per Capita 1970 (Zero-Order Correlations)

	Felony Crime Rates		
	Total	Personal	Property
Demographic Characteristics (N=32)			
Percent Urban	.38*	.37*	.38*
Unemployment	-.06	-.05	-.06
Overcrowded Housing	-.16	-.08	-.16
Poverty	-.18	-.09	-.18
Inequality (% Black)	.71***	.72***	.70***
Percent Males 25-29 yrs.	.43**	.39*	.43**
Percent Males under 19 yrs.	-.54**	-.46**	-.54**
Criminal Justice Resources (N=20)			
Police Expenditures	.90***	.92***	.89***
Police Personnel	.89***	.91***	.88***
Prosecutor Expenditures	.03	.0	.03
Prosecutor Personnel	-.26	-.18	-.27
Superior Court Expenditures	.54**	.58**	.53**
Superior Court Personnel	.69***	.61**	.69***

Sources: Bureau of Criminal Statistics and Special Services, County Criminal Justice Profiles;
U.S. Bureau of the Census, City and County Databook (1970); California Bureau of
Finance (unpublished mimeographs).

*p<.05   **p<.01   ***p<.001

implications for the generation of punishment, since the highly discretionary role of the prosecutor in bringing or dropping charges
against the defendant, examining the facts of the case, bargaining for
reduced charges, and influencing the method of case disposition (dismissal, guilty plea, or trial) will likely be affected by organizational
caseloads. For example, high caseloads due to disproportionate police
resources and high recorded crime rates may diminish the court's
capacity to mete out swift, certain, and severe punishments—
conditions thought to be necessary for a deterrent influence of criminal punishment. The absence of an association between crime rate
and prosecutorial resources may therefore indicate a condition that is

favorable to court overload and a diminished capacity to generate and administer legal sanctions.

Criminal Justice Resources

Relationships between criminal justice resources and selected demographic characteristics of California counties are shown in table 2. The greatest positive correlations are between percent black and police resources, in terms of both personnel and expenditures. More urban counties and those with large percentages of males between 25 and 29 years of age also appear to have greater police resources. In addition, counties with higher concentrations of males below 19 years of age spend less for police, as well as for felony courts. Inequality also shows a weak negative association ($-.33$) with prosecutorial personnel per capita.

Although some associations are shown, particularly with police resources, the selected demographic characteristics show little influence on prosecutorial and judicial resources or capacity. Police agencies are the most publicly visible of all criminal justice components and are thus more likely to receive additional funding when a rise in crime is perceived. The increased capacity of the police to record and detect criminal activities may itself help produce increases in recorded crimes.[3] Demographic characteristics, especially inequality and urbanization, are moderately related to both crime and police resources and are not associated with expenditures for prosecution or the judiciary—those components of the criminal justice system which must sort out violators and apply sanctions to convicted defendants.

There are three possible reasons for this finding, one of which has already been mentioned, namely, the relatively low public visibility of both the prosecutor's office and the superior court. Another possible explanation is that the police, unlike prosecutors or the judiciary, are funded primarily at the municipal level. Police resource levels will, therefore, be more responsive to a changing social environment, while other agency budgets are relatively fixed through county and state legislation.

A third possible reason for this apparent lack of court funding relative to police spending may have to do with public and legislative folkwisdom concerning "crime control." Putting more cops on the

TABLE 2 Demographic Characteristics of California Counties by Criminal
Justice Resources Per Capita 1970 (Zero-Order Correlations, N = 32)

Demographic Characteristics	Police		Prosecutor		Superior Court	
	Spending	Personnel	Spending	Personnel	Spending	Personnel
Percent Urban	.55***	.33*	-.01	-.17	.17	-.02
Unemployment	-.27	-.12	.08	.05	-.15	.20
Overcrowded Housing	-.15	.07	-.05	-.09	-.15	-.23
Poverty	-.38*	-.20	-.06	.08	-.25	-.08
Inequality (% Black)	.66***	.60***	-.11	-.33*	.27	.12
Percent Males 25-29 Years	.44**	.34**	-.17	-.15	.21	.07
Percent Males under 19 Years	-.47**	-.34*	.03	.18	-.29*	-.51**

Sources: Bureau of Criminal Statistics and Special Services, County Criminal Justice Profiles; U.S. Bureau of the Census, City and County Databook (1970); California Bureau of Finance (unpublished mimeographs).

*p<.05   **p<.01   ***p<.001

beat may appear most effective in the short run for the control of certain criminal activities. People generally feel that an increased police presence will deter some criminals, although this has never been conclusively shown through research.[4] Be that as it may, without commensurate increases in capacity for those legal institutions that back up police authority, namely, courts and prisons, less frequent, less certain, and less severe punishments may result for those apprehended, because of system overload. This may indeed help undermine both the purpose of increased police presence (deterrence) and general respect for legal authority and norms, without which legal punishments cannot be effective as deterrents to crime. This idea of "imbalance" in organizational resource allocations, and its relationship to both court caseloads and criminal sanctioning, are discussed in the following sections.

COURT CASELOAD

As stated earlier, resource discrepancies in the criminal justice system, especially between police agencies and prosecutor's offices, may affect the generation and administration of criminal sanctions. Potential court caseload pressure is measured here in relation to three factors: (1) the resources of police and prosecutorial components (the ratio of police resources to prosecutorial resources); (2) superior court dispositions per capita; and (3) felony arrest rate. It is assumed that these variables will affect actual court caseloads and the system's capacity to sanction violators. High arrest rates, large resource differences, and a high level of dispositions per capita may provide favorable conditions for court overload. *Actual* court caseload is measured in relation to the number of superior court dispositions per prosecutorial resource in terms of personnel.

The correlations for the measures of potential and actual court workload pressure, demographic characteristics, criminal justice resources, and rates of felony crimes are presented in table 3. These are discussed in the following four sections.

Criminal Justice Resources and Potential Court Caseload
Felony arrests represent potential cases in superior courts. As could be expected, strong relationships are observed between levels of

police spending and personnel and felony arrest rate (.86 and .87 respectively). Thus, counties with high police resource levels are also likely to have high rates of arrests. The correlations between superior court resources and felony arrest rates are moderate (.54 for both court spending and court personnel per capita). While judicial resources are positively related to arrest rate, no significant association is observed for prosecutorial resources; in fact, the signs of the correlations are negative.

Another measure of potential court caseload pressure, dispositions per capita, shows moderate positive associations with police resources (.49 for spending and .56 for personnel), a weak positive correlation (.32) with superior court spending, and a weak negative association with prosecutorial personnel ($-.30$). Thus, counties with high numbers of superior court dispositions per capita are likely to have relatively high police resources but not prosecutorial and judicial resources.

A third measure of potential caseload pressure is the ratio of police resources to prosecutorial resources. It was earlier hypothesized that counties in which this ratio is high may have greater actual caseload pressure due to higher inputs of alleged violators into court systems which must dispose of them. As shown in table 3, greater police expenditure and personnel levels are likely to produce more discrepancy between police and prosecutorial resources. The correlation between this discrepancy, or "imbalance," and police spending is .69; for police personnel it is .65. As might be expected, counties with relatively low expenditures for prosecutors are likely to have a greater imbalance between police and prosecutor resources ($-.55$ for prosecutorial spending and $-.58$ for prosecutorial personnel). A low to moderate positive correlation exists between police-prosecutor imbalance and superior court personnel (.40).

Criminal Justice Resources and Court Caseload

Workload pressure in the superior court is measured here as the number of dispositions in 1970 per prosecutorial personnel. Police resources in terms of both expenditures and personnel per capita are positively related to court pressure (.61 and .48 respectively). Jurisdictions with low levels of prosecutorial resources per capita are more likely to have greater caseloads than those with more prosecuting

TABLE 3 Potential and Actual Court Caseload Pressure by Rates of Felony
Crime, Criminal Justice Resources Per Capita, and Demographic Characteristics 1970
(Zero-Order Correlations)

	Potential Court Caseload Pressure			Actual Court Caseload Pressure
	Total Felony Arrest Rate	Court Dispositions Per Capita	Police-Prosecutor Resource Imbalance	Dispositions per Prosecutorial Personnel
Criminal Justice Resources per capita (N=35)				
Police Spending	.86***	.49***	.69***	.61***
Police Personnel	.87***	.56***	.65***	.48**
Prosecutor Spending	-.12	-.03	-.55***	-.56***
Prosecutor Personnel	-.20	-.30*	-.58***	-.53***
Court Spending	.54***	.32*	.25	.35*
Court Personnel	.54***	.09	.40**	-.07
Demographic Characteristic (N=36)				
Percent Urban	.43***	.01	.41**	.15
Unemployment	-.12	.16	-.17	.15

Overcrowded Housing	-.12	.32*	-.07	.22
Poverty	-.19	.17	-.16	-.01
Inequality (% Black)	.66***	.46***	.70***	.54***
Percent Males 25-29 yrs.	.52***	.15	.58***	.20
Percent Males under 19 yrs.	-.35**	.09	-.34**	-.01
Felony Crime Rates (N=22)				
Total	.80***	.42*	.71***	.50**
Personal	.86***	.60***	.70***	.60***
Property	.79***	.40*	.71***	.49***

Sources: Bureau of Criminal Statistics and Special Services, County Criminal Justice Profiles; U.S. Bureau of the Census, City and County Databook (1970); California Bureau of Finance (unpublished mimeographs).

*p<.05 **p<.01 ***p<.001

resources (− .56 for expenditures and − .53 for personnel). Judicial spending shows a weak positive association (.35) with court caseload. These results generally replicate those found for police-prosecutor imbalance and workload pressure. The greater the proportion of criminal justice resources given to police agencies, the greater both the potential caseload (in terms of felony arrests, police-prosecutorial imbalance, and dispositions) and the actual workload pressure in felony courts.

Demographic Characteristics, Criminal
Justice Resources, and Court Caseload

Of all demographic characteristics measured, inequality, measured here as the percent black, shows the highest and most consistent positive correlations with both potential and actual court caseload pressure (see table 3). For felony arrest rate the correlation is .66, followed by other population characteristics of percentage of males aged 25 to 29 (.52) and urbanization (.43). A negative relation is found between arrest rate and percentage of males below 19 years of age (− .35). Inequality also shows the highest correlation with police-prosecutor resources (.70), followed by males aged 25 to 29 (.58) and urbanization (.41). Only two demographic characteristics, inequality and overcrowded housing, are positively associated with superior court dispositions per capita (.46 and .32 respectively). The only positive, significant correlation with actual court caseload pressure is found for inequality (.54).

Thus, of all demographic characteristics of counties measured, inequality, defined here as the percent black in the population, is the most consistently related to both potential and actual court workload pressure.

Crime Rates, Criminal Justice Resources, and Court Caseload

Felony crime rates, for both personal and property crimes, show moderate to high correlations with potential and actual court caseload pressure. The highest associations are found for felony arrest rate (.80 total crimes, .86 personal crimes, and .79 property crimes). Thus, counties with high crime rates also have high arrest rates, which produces a situation of potential overload for criminal courts. Crime rates are also highly associated with police-prosecutor resource imbalance. It was shown earlier that while crime rates were highly associated with police resources and moderately related to judicial expenditures and personnel, they were not related to prosecutorial resources. The association between felony crime rates and police-prosecutor imbalance is rather strong (.70 for personal felony crime rate and .71 for total and property felony crime rates).

Rates of crime are moderately associated with another measure of potential caseload, felony court dispositions per capita. The highest association is found for personal felony crime rate (.60), followed by total crime rate (.42) and property crimes (.40). Thus, crime rate is also related to potential court workload pressure as measured by felony dispositions per capita.

Finally, felony crime rates show moderate positive correlations with actual court caseload pressure. The highest association is found for personal felony crimes (.60).

These results indicate that jurisdictions with high rates of reported felony crimes are likely to have greater caseload pressure in their felony courts. This appears to be true despite high rates of case dismissals in crime-prone areas—as high as 50 percent of all cases filed—reported in previous research.[5] Thus, even with such "safety-valve institutions" as police and prosecutor dismissing privileges, areas with high reported crime rates are likely to have greater caseloads in their felony courts.

COURT PROCESSING

Conviction and Plea Bargaining

It is already documented that a large proportion of cases in the nation's criminal courts are disposed through pleas of guilty.[6] Plea bargaining enables courts to move large caseloads, but at the expense of lowered rates of sanctioning. That is, pleading guilty to a lesser charge will generally bring less punishment to bear on a defendant than if he were found guilty on the original charge.

Some have argued that as court caseloads increase, there is a decline in adversariness in processing cases, as prosecutors encourage plea bargaining in order to keep cases moving.[7] Increased cooperation is required between defense attorneys and prosecutors in order for this to occur. The "demise of the adversary system" is a label applied to this type of criminal processing by those who view such "cooperation" negatively. Plea bargaining, it is argued, indicates a less adversarial procedure, threatening a major tenet of due process in the justice system.

Conversely, others argue that adversariness in criminal cases has not declined.[8] Plea bargaining is not a recent phenomenon in criminal courts. It has been the major method of case disposition for decades[9] and has not been drastically augmented in the past ten years as a response to an ever-increasing crime rate.

Thus, the relationship between caseload and adversariness in the criminal court is still a topic of debate among legal scholars. The ecological correlates of methods of case disposition are presented in table 4.

It has already been shown that the conviction rate (the ratio of convictions to dispositions) is, on the average, close to 90 percent. Only three factors show weak yet significant correlations with this variable (see table 4): urbanization (.32), superior court personnel per capita (−.32), and dispositions per capita (−.34). This may be the product of an initial screening by the court, which leaves only those cases likely to be disposed by conviction within the system. Thus, conviction rates are likely to be high regardless of caseload pressures, criminal justice resources, rates of reported crimes, and inequality. It should be noted, however, that a finer breakdown of court conviction rates, by specific offense charged, may produce different results than found here. The composition of cases, or the "case mix," undoubtedly influences the overall rate of conviction.[10]

Almost all criminal court convictions are obtained through plea bargaining. The means of conviction—original guilty plea, changed plea of guilty, and tried guilty—as well as total guilty pleas are shown in table 4. Original ("fast") guilty pleas can be taken as representing a less adversarial proceeding than other means of conviction.

Since almost all cases ae disposed through bargaining in criminal courts, it is unreasonable to assume that only trials show adversariness.[11] A more meaningful measure appears to be how the case was bargained: with speed (original guilty plea), or more slowly (changed to guilty plea). Of course, trials represent the most adversarial proceeding, so they, too, can be taken as a measure of conflict between the state and the defense.

It could be argued that fast guilty pleas will result in higher sanctioning rates, since less ground is given by the state in terms of reducing original charges. Defendants who plead guilty immediately are likely to be convicted of the offense originally charged, which will carry a higher maximum penalty than will a reduced charge. Where trial rates are high, one can also expect higher rates of punishment. Most criminal trials end in convictions on more serious charges than those offered through bargaining. Defendants with prior records and those charged with serious offenses will be more likely to go to trial, as the "bargains" in their cases usually carry a prison term. Rather than pleading guilty, these defendants will be more likely to take their chances at trial.[12] If convicted at trial, however (which is usually the case), these defendants will be penalized more severely than if they had pleaded guilty.

Prosecutors do not desire to go to trial for ordinary criminal cases, as this leads to a greater expenditure of scarce resources (time and personnel) and adds an element of uncertainty, which reduces their control over the conviction process; in other words, not *all* trials result in a verdict of guilty. It must also be remembered that the image of the prosecutor as "protector of the public" is measured by his or her track record concerning convictions. Trials waste time and will appear to make a court less efficient in convicting offenders—an important occupational consideration, since the prosecutor is an elected official.

As seen in table 4, the total rate of guilty pleas in superior courts shows no significant correlations with rates of felony crimes, demographic characteristics of jurisdictions, or criminal justice resources. A weak negative association ($-.34$) is observed for dispositions per capita, a measure of potential court overload. The more court dispositions relative to the population at large, the less likely it is for the court to have a high rate of guilty pleas. While this association is weak, it does not support the notion that high rates of plea bargaining are due to caseload pressures. Again, the data may not be fine enough (i.e., offense-specific) to reveal ecological associations with the rate of plea bargaining, but the results are not in line with the hypothesis that caseloads reduce adversariness in felony courts.

Rates of tried guilty cases show only two weak correlations in table 4. These are with inequality (.36) and rate of personal felony crimes (.35). While trial rates do not vary with most factors measured, it is

TABLE 4 Means of Conviction and Conviction Rate in Superior Court
by Demographic Characteristics, Criminal Justice Resources, Rates of
Felony Crimes, and Potential and Actual Caseload Pressure 1970
(Zero-Order Correlations)

	Conviction Rate	Original Guilty Plea	Changed to Guilty Plea	Tried Guilty	Total Guilty Pleas
Demographic Characteristics (N=33)					
Percent Urban	.32*	-.52***	.52***	.07	.07
Unemployment	-.17	.49**	-.43**	-.12	.07
Overcrowded Housing	-.09	.29*	-.29*	-.05	0
Poverty	-.24	.43**	-.53***	.09	-.17
Inequality (% Black)	-.01	-.34*	.16	.36*	-.25
Percent Males 25-29 yrs.	.10	-.28	.25	.07	-.03
Percent Males under 19 yrs.	-.23	.23	-.16	-.18	0
Criminal Justice Resources (N=35)					
Police Spending	.14	-.23	.19	.11	.01
Police Personnel	-.11	-.10	.06	.08	-.12

Prosecutor Spending	-.01	.09	-.03	-.19	.08
Prosecutor Personnel	-.06	.36*	-.42**	0	-.07
Court Spending	-.24	-.18	.15	.10	-.21
Court Personnel	-.32*	.25	-.28*	-.02	-.18
Felony Crime Rates (N=25)					
Total	.08	-.06	.04	.02	.02
Personal	-.15	-.21	0	.35*	-.31
Property	.10	-.04	.05	0	.05
Potential and Actual Caseload Pressure (N=36)					
Felony Arrest Rate	-.05	-.08	-.04	.22	-.16
Dispositions per capita	-.34*	-.04	-.07	.27	-.34*
Police-Prosecutor					
Resource Imbalance	.14	-.17	.12	.16	0
Court Dispositions					
per Prosecutor Personnel	-.11	-.26	.23	.20	-.13

Sources: Bureau of Criminal Statistics and Special Services, County Criminal Justice Profiles; U.S. Bureau of the Census, City and County Databook (1970); California Bureau of Finance (unpublished mimeographs).

*p<.05   **p<.01   ***p<.001

interesting to note the consistently positive signs of these low correlations with measures of potential and actual caseload pressure. This is in contrast to the consistently negative signs for original guilty pleas with these same factors. While not highly supportive, these patterns suggest that where potential and actual caseloads are higher, there may be *more* adversarial court proceedings than where such pressures are low. This appears to question further the notion that courts under greater caseload pressure are less adversarial in processing defendants.

Original and changed to guilty plea disposition rates are highly inversely correlated. That is, where one is high, the other will be low. The correlations obtained in table 4 reflect this pattern; original ("fast") pleas of guilty show significant relations with ecological factors, and changed ("slow") pleas show a correlation of similar magnitude but of the opposite sign.

Urban jurisdictions show lower rates of fast guilty pleas and correspondingly higher rates of slow or changed pleas. Inequality displays a weak negative association with fast guilty pleas and a weak positive association with the rate of defendants tried and found guilty. Unemployment, overcrowded housing, and poverty show weak to moderate positive correlations with fast guilty pleas and corresponding negative correlations with slow pleas. Thus, population measures associated with economic deprivation and powerlessness are positively associated with rates of fast pleas in criminal courts—the least adversarial means of case disposition. This may be indicative of less representation of the poor, who are encouraged by both prosecution and defense to plead guilty early in their cases.[13]

Prosecutorial personnel per capita is also significantly related to type of guilty plea in superior court. The higher the prosecutorial personnel per capita, the greater the rate of fast guilty pleas (.36) and the lower the rate of slow guilty pleas (-.42). Contrary to what might be expected, where prosecutorial resources are relatively scarce, more adversarial proceedings may occur as measured by cases disposed through slow guilty pleas.

Overall, table 4 shows few significant correlations with conviction and guilty plea rates in superior courts. An exception to this is found for demographic characteristics of jurisdictions; measures of general economic deprivation appear to be positively associated with fast disposal of cases through original guilty pleas. Moreover, potential and actual caseload pressure show no consistent or significant relations with means of conviction, and, in fact, the signs of the relations suggest that caseload pressure is negatively related to fast processing of felony cases. Thus, it may be that where caseload pressure is greatest, more adversarial proceedings will occur, in terms of both fewer original guilty pleas and more trials in criminal courts. The associations between these variables and sentencing rates are discussed in the following section.

CRIMINAL SANCTIONING

Demographic Characteristics

Table 5 presents correlations for sentencing probabilities, measured by the ratio of the number of a particular type of sentence to total dispositions in superior court. The percentage of felony convictions of all dispositions is also included. These measures do not represent punishments actually carried out, but only sentencing outcomes. As mentioned earlier, the number of suspended sentences was not available from this data set.

The rate of prison sentencing in superior courts, the most severe sentencing outcome, is most highly correlated with poverty (.51) and unemployment (.42) of all characteristics of jurisdictions measured. A weak negative association is observed for urbanization (− .32). These same demographic features showed similar relationships to original or fast guilty plea rates, which in turn could be related to more severe sentencing, due, at least in part, to the unlikely dropping of charges.

Demographic characteristics show no significant relationships to incarceration rates (jail and prison sentences combined) or to sentences of probation with jail. Unemployment is the only factor related to rate of jail sentences, and this is in the weak range (.38). Similarly, inequality is the only factor measured that is related to straight probation sentencing (.32).

Thus, of all sentencing outcomes, the rate of prison sentencing shows the greatest relationship to population characteristics. Furthermore, the finding of more severe sentencing (prison) in areas of relatively high unemployment and poverty suggests a close connection

TABLE 5 Superior Court Sentencing Rates by Demographic Characteristics, Criminal Justice Resources, Rates of Felony Crimes, Means of Conviction, and Potential and Actual Caseload Pressure 1970 (Zero-Order Correlations)

			Sentencing Rates			
	Prison	Incarceration[a]	Jail Only	Probation and Jail	Probation Only	Felony Conviction
Demographic Characteristics (N=33)						
Percent Urban	-.32*	-.20	-.23	.05	.15	.09
Unemployment	.42**	.15	.38*	-.21	.01	-.17
Overcrowded Housing	.12	-.07	.08	-.15	-.06	-.21
Poverty	.51***	.19	-.02	-.02	-.24	.06
Inequality (% Black)	-.19	-.27	-.02	-.15	.32*	-.11
Percent Males 25-29 yrs.	.07	-.03	-.11	-.13	.10	.01
Percent Males under 19 yrs.	-.26	-.02	-.15	-.12	.07	-.30*

Criminal Justice
Resources
(N=35)

Police Spending	-.26	-.27	-.07	-.07	.27	.06
Police Personnel	-.21	-.33*	.11	-.26	.32*	-.12
Prosecutor Spending	.03	.01	.36*	-.24	.15	-.08
Prosecutor Personnel	.17	.16	.15	-.04	-.08	.07
Court Spending	-.06	-.33*	.03	-.27	.27	-.16
Court Personnel	.03	.02	.25	-.16	.01	-.19
Potential and Actual Caseload Pressure						
Police-Prosecutor Resource Imbalance (N=26)	-.26	-.46**	-.35 *	-.12	.37*	0
Disposition per Prosector Personnel (N=35)	-.39**	-.45**	.14	-.31	.41**	-.45**

Sentencing Rates

	Prison	Incarceration[a]	Jail Only	Probation and Jail	Probation Only	Felony Conviction
Felony Crime Rates (N=25)						
Total	-.20	-.17	-.14	.01	.16	.11
Personal	-.27	-.37*	-.06	-.16	.32	-.07
Property	-.19	-.16	-.14	.02	.15	.12
Means of Conviction (N=42)						
Conviction Rate	-.17	-.03	-.22	.17	.02	.51***
Original Guilty Plea	.39*	.25*	.06	.02	-.14	.16
Changed to Guilty Plea	-.43*	-.18	.0	.02	.07	-.11
Tried Guilty	-.01	-.19	-.13	-.08	.17	-.13
Total Guilty Pleas	-.10	.10	-.04	.15	-.08	.37***

Sources: Bureau of Criminal Statistics and Special Services, County Criminal Justice Profiles;

U.S. Bureau of the Census, City and County Databook (1970); California Bureau of

Finance (unpublished mimeographs).

aPrison and jail sentences combined.

*p<.05   **p<.01   ***p<.001

between economic conditions and sanctioning activities of felony courts, corroborating the theories of Rusche and Kirchheimer[14] concerning economic conditions and punishment, and of Christie[15] in terms of the likelihood of increased punishment when its value is depressed by living conditions of the population.

These findings are congruent with those found earlier concerning means of conviction. Measures of economic deprivation were related to the fast disposition of felony cases (measured by original pleas of guilty). These same measures of deprivation are related to more severe sentencing in criminal courts. This suggests that in a population where defendants are likely to bring fewer resources to bear on their cases, faster processing and more severe punishment will result.

Criminal Sanctioning and Criminal Justice Resources

As shown in table 5, superior court sentencing displays only a few significant correlations with criminal justice resource levels. Police personnel per capita shows a weak negative correlation with sentencing rates carrying incarceration ($-.33$) and a weak positive association with probation sentencing ($.32$). The signs of the correlations between both police expenditures and personnel per capita and rate of prison sentencing are both negative ($-.26$ and $-.21$ respectively), possibly indicating an overload phenomenon, which leads to a lowered rate of incarceration. Similarly, police expenditures per capita show a negative association with sentences of incarceration ($-.27$) and a positive association with probation sentencing ($.27$).

Prosecutorial spending per capita is positively related to sentences of jail only ($.36$), and judicial expenditures show a weak negative association with sentences of incarceration ($-.33$). None of the resource variables measured are related to the rate of felony sentences, probation with jail sentences, or prison sentences. For the latter, police resources show very weak negative correlations which are not significant.

Criminal Sanctioning, Resource Imbalance, and Court Caseload

The degree of imbalance between police and prosecutor resources, a measure of potential court overload, displays weak to moderate correlations with rates of court sentencing. It is negatively related to sentences carrying incarceration ($-.46$), jail only sentences ($-.35$), and prison sentencing ($-.26$, $p > .05$). It also shows a weak positive association with straight probation sentencing (.37). Thus, it appears that the greater the resource differential between these two criminal justice components, the less likely it is for convicted felons to receive harsh punishments.

This relationship is corroborated by the results found for actual caseload pressure, measured as the ratio of dispositions to prosecutorial personnel. Caseload pressure is negatively associated with sentences of incarceration (−.45), felony sentences (−.45), prison (−.39), and probation with jail (−.31). It is related positively to sentences of probation only (.41). Thus, courts with high caseloads appear less likely to impose severe sentences on defendants.

The correlations between both potential and actual caseload pressure and rates of punishments produced by superior courts suggest that punishment may indeed be responsive to overloading of the court system. The data show a weak to moderate negative relation between relatively harsh punishments and caseload. In fact, *of all variables shown in table 5, potential and actual caseloads are the most consistently related to rates of criminal sanctioning.*

The possible effect of caseload on sentencing does not appear to be mediated by increased plea bargaining. Neither potential nor actual caseload pressure is consistently related to means of conviction or guilty plea rate in the felony court. Court dispositions per capita are actually *negatively* related to the rate of guilty pleas.

The connection between caseload and final punishment meted out by the courts is thus problematic. Court caseload does not appear to increase the proportion of guilty pleas, which would, in turn, lessen the certainty of statutory punishments.

A possible answer to this paradox is that the *rate* of guilty pleas need not increase from burgeoning caseloads in order for caseloads to have an effect on punishment. It is possible that the entire penalty structure, or "going rate" of punishment in criminal courts, is reduced by large numbers of defendants. Backlogged cases, jammed detention facilities, and crowded and inadequate prisons may necessitate "better deals" by the prosecution during the bargaining process.

Thus, the content of these "deals" in terms of reduced charges and promises of leniency may be equally, or more, important than mere rates of negotiated cases. Unfortunately, this cannot be tested with the data at hand. It appears likely that the *qualitative aspects* of bargains struck between defense and prosecution go far in explaining the relationship between caseload and criminal sanctioning. Caseload may lower penalty structures used to bargain cases, but it does not appear to affect the proportion of such cases in criminal courts. The justice meted out under circumstances of relatively high caseloads is not necessarily less adversarial in nature. Thus, the "demise of the adversary system" is probably a less accurate portrayal of what is happening to criminal courts than a "demise of statutory punishment."

Criminal Sanctioning and Means of Conviction

The rate of original pleas of guilty displays a weak yet positive relation to harsh sentencing (see table 5). Under such circumstances, court systems that have relatively high numbers of cases disposed of by original, or fast guilty pleas, also have higher rates of both prison and incarceration sentencing (.39 and .25, respectively). Changed, or slow rates of guilty pleas show a negative association with prison sentencing ($-.43$). A positive association exists between total guilty plea rate and felony convictions (.37). In addition, those courts with high conviction rates are also likely to have a high proportion of felony convictions (.51).

These relationships generally support the notion that court adversariness negatively affects punishment levels. Cases that are processed with relative speed (i.e., by original guilty pleas) may more plausibly result in harsh punishment for the defendant. Of course, various characteristics of an individual case certainly play a role in both the means of disposition and the punishment or lack thereof.

The data show that court systems with higher rates of relatively adversarial proceedings (slow guilty pleas) are also likely to have lowered rates of criminal sanctioning. Whether this is due to the types of cases or "case-mix" cannot be determined, but a probable explanation for the pattern is that charges are more often dropped in cases disposed of through prolonged bargaining. A changed plea by the defendant frequently hinges upon a reduction of charges or a promise of lenient sentencing.

Criminal Sanctioning and Rates of Crime

A weak negative correlation is found between the rate of personal felony crimes and the rate of sentences carrying incarceration ($-.37$). It is interesting to note that while the correlations are not significant, the signs of the associations between rates of felony crimes and both incarceration and prison sentences are negative. For rates of straight probation sentencing, the correlations show positive signs. In light of the preceding findings of positive correlations among crime, police resources, and court overload, the associations between crime rates and punishment levels are not surprising. These correlations seem hardly supportive of a deterrent effect of punishment on crime. In contradistinction, they evidence how rates of crime may overburden legal machinery, resulting in lowered penalty structures.[16]

Extended Analyses

The preceding analysis of zero-order (Pearson product-moment) correlations presents only a limited picture of the possible relationships among crime, law, and society. In order to examine these associations more fully, partial correlations will be employed.[17] Partial correlations allow an examination of the relationship between two variables while "controlling" for the effects of other variables. Such an analysis will identify those bi-variate relationships that are "spurious," or due to a common third cause, and associations that may be mediated by an intervening variable.[18]

Table 6 presents partial correlations among demographic characteristics, police spending, and total felony crime rate. The correlation between percent urban and crime rate (.38, see table 1) is significantly reduced when inequality and percent of males 25 to 29 years of age are separately controlled (to .14 and .17 respectively). When this relation (percent urban to crime rate) is controlled for police spending, it becomes negative ($-.33$). The correlation between percent males 25 to 29 years and crime rate (.43) is also substantially reduced when controlled for other variables (see table 6). In contrast, the relation between inequality and crime rate (.71) is not reduced significantly except for police resources. When police resources are controlled, the relation between inequality and crime is only .21. This may indicate an intervening influence of police spending. In other words, inequality may increase police spending, which, in turn, may produce higher reported crime. The correlation between police spending and crime rate (.90) remains significant when demographic controls are added. The largest decrease is noted when percent males aged 25 to 29 is controlled, producing a partial correlation of .39. Thus, of all possible

TABLE 6 Felony Crime Rate by Selected Independent and Control
Variables 1970 (Partial Correlations)

Controls (N=20)	Independent Variables			
	Percent Urban	Inequality	Percent Males Aged 25-29	Police Spending
Percent Urban	--	.65***	.25	.90***
Inequality	.14	--	.13	.72***
Percent Males aged 25-29	.17	.64***	--	.39*
Police Spending	-.33	.21	.08	--

Sources: Bureau of Criminal Statistics and Special Services, County Criminal Justice Profiles;

U.S. Bureau of the Census, City and County Databook (1970); California Bureau of

Finance (unpublished mimeographs).

*p<.05   ***p<.001

determinants of crime, inequality and police spending show significant positive associations when other variables are controlled. The effects of inequality are reduced significantly, however, when police resources are controlled, indicating a possible mediating influence of this latter variable.

Table 7 presents additional data that bear on these findings. The partial correlation between inequality and crime is reduced to .21 when police spending is controlled and is .18 when police personnel is controlled. Since it is unlikely that police resources "cause" inequality, it is plausible that it is an intervening influence. However, when the relation between inequality, measured by percent black in the population, and police resources is controlled for crime, the association is also reduced but remains significantly positive for police personnel (.35). There is a weak relation between police personnel and inequality *regardless* of the amount of crime. Thus, it is possible that police resources provide an intervening link between inequality and crime. Where there are relatively high amounts of inequality, more police are deployed, regardless of the reported crime rate. More police presence may lead to an increase in reported crimes due to the increased official capacity to record and detect it.[19]

Table 8 reinforces this finding. The associations between inequality

TABLE 7 Inequality by Police Resources and Felony Crime Rate 1970
(Partial Correlations)

Controls (N=20)	Felony Crime	Police Spending	Police Personnel
Felony Crime	--	.29	.35*
Police Spending	.21	--	--
Police Personnel	.18	--	--

Source: Bureau of Criminal Statistics and Special Services, County Criminal
         Justice Profiles.

*p<.05

and police resources remain essentially unaffected when percent urban and percent males aged 25 to 29 are controlled. Table 9 displays partial correlations between criminal justice resources and felony crime rate when controls for selected demographic characteristics are introduced. The original associations remain unaffected except for a slight reduction between police resources and crime rate when inequality is controlled. Inequality does not "explain away" this relation, but does reduce it slightly. In addition, the correlation of .54 between superior court expenditures and crime is reduced to .23 when inequality is controlled. While these data do not indicate the causal direction of the relationship between crime and criminal justice resources, they do indicate that the relationship remains largely unaffected by population characteristics. Where there are more police, there are more reported crimes, regardless of population characteristics. However, there is a reduction in the association between both police spending and personnel and crime rate when inequality is controlled (from .90 to .72 and from .89 to .68, respectively).

Table 10 displays the partial correlations among criminal justice resource levels and actual caseload pressure, controlling for measures of potential pressure. For police resources, the relationships are greatly reduced, indicating a possible mediating influence of potential pressure in the relationship between police resources and court caseload pressure. Increased police resources are likely to create a

TABLE 8 Police Spending and Personnel by Selected Independent and
Control Variables 1970 (Partial Correlations)

| | Independent Variables | | | | | |
| | Police Spending | | | Police Personnel | | |
Controls (N=24)	Percent Urban	Inequality	Percent Males 25-29 yrs.	Percent Urban	Inequality	Percent Males 25-29 yrs.
Percent Urban	---	.64***	.35*	---	.67***	.36*
Inequality	.48**	---	.45*	.32	---	.39*
Percent Males 25-29 yrs.	.37*	.63***	---	.24	.66***	---

Sources: Bureau of Criminal Statistics and Special Services, County Criminal Justice Profiles;

U.S. Bureau of the Census, City and County Databook (1970); California Bureau of

Finance (unpublished mimeographs).

*p<.05   **p<.01   ***p<.001

TABLE 9 Felony Crime Rate by Criminal Justice Resources Controlled for
Demographic Characteristics 1970 (Partial Correlations)

	Criminal Justice Resources							
	Police		Prosecutor		Superior Court			
Controls (N=20)	Spending	Personnel	Spending	Personnel	Spending	Personnel		
Percent Urban	.91***	.87***	.02	-.29	.41*	.64***		
Unemployment	.91***	.89***	.04	-.26	.54**	.69***		
Poverty	.90***	.88***	.02	-.25	.52**	.69***		
Inequality	.72***	.68***	.05	-.09	.23	.59**		
Percent Males								
25-29 yrs	.88***	.86***	.14	-.24	.38	.59**		

Sources: Bureau of Criminal Statistics and Special Services, County Criminal Justice Profiles;
U.S. Bureau of the Census, City and County Databook (1970); California Bureau of
Finance (unpublished mimeographs).

*p<.05 **p<.01 ***p<.001

TABLE 10 Court Caseload Pressure by Criminal Justice Resources
Controlled for Potential Court Caseload Pressure 1970
(Partial Correlations)

| | Criminal Justice Resources | | | | | |
| | Police | | Prosecutor | | Superior Court | |
Controls (N=35)	Spending	Personnel	Spending	Personnel	Spending	Personnel
Felony Arrest Rate	.03	.08	-.21	-.69***	-.13	-.33
Police-Prosecutor Resource Imbalance	.06	.16	.25	-.44*	.08	.27
Court Dispositions per capita	.22	.12	-.44*	-.90***	-.12	.04

Source: Bureau of Criminal Statistics and Special Services, County Criminal Justice Profiles.

*p<.05 **p<.01 ***p<.001

condition of potential court caseload pressure, which, in turn, leads to increased court caseloads. In contrast, the negative relation between prosecutor resources and caseload remains, and for personnel levels is substantially increased when disposition per capita is controlled ($-.90$). Thus, where there are relatively less prosecuting resources, greater caseloads for the prosecutor will exist, despite conditions of potential court overload.

Controlling for demographic influences does not significantly alter the relationships among resource levels and caseload pressure, with the exception of inequality. When inequality is controlled, the relationship between police resources and caseload pressure disappears, indicating a spurious relationship. Thus, it appears that inequality affects both police resources and court caseload pressure and may be responsible for the observed relation between the latter two variables.

Table 11 displays the partial correlations among demographic characteristics and measures of potential caseload pressure, namely, felony arrest rate and police-prosecutor resource imbalance. Inequality remains significantly related to potential caseload pressure, when other demographic influences are controlled. It is reduced the most when police resources are controlled. The relationship between urbanization and potential court caseload disappears when other demographic characteristics are controlled. Percent males aged 25 to 29 remains associated with potential caseload when population characteristics are controlled but is significantly reduced when police resources are controlled, pointing to a possible intervening influence of police resources. It is interesting to note that although the relationship between inequality and police-prosecutor resource imbalance is reduced when police resources are controlled, the relation remains significantly positive. Thus, where inequality is greater, potential court caseload is likely to be greater, despite police spending levels.

The original finding of no significant correlations between court caseload pressure and means of conviction is not changed when demographic factors are controlled.

The partial correlations among crime, inequality, police resources, and caseload pressure are displayed in table 12. Inequality remains positively related to caseload pressure when police resources are controlled. However, it is reduced from .54 to .30 when crime is controlled. The relationship between police resources and court caseload pressure (.61 for police spending and .48 for police personnel) disap-

TABLE 11 Selected Demographic Characteristics by Potential Court Caseload Controlled for Demographic Characteristics and Police Resources 1970 (Partial Correlations)

| | Potential Court Caseload | | | | | |
| | Felony Arrest Rate | | | Police-Prosecutor Resource Imbalance | | |
Controls (N=35)	Inequality	Percent Urban	Percent Males 25-29 yrs.	Inequality	Percent Urban	Percent Males 25-29 yrs.
Percent Urban	.63***	--	.39*	.65***	--	.51**
Inequality	--	.22	.37*	--	.12	.45*
Percent Males						
25-29 yrs.	.61***	.15	--	.61***	-.01	--
Police Spending	.25	-.17	.09	.36*	-.15	.28
Police Personnel	.20	.02	.16	.37*	.02	.34

Sources: Bureau of Criminal Statistics and Special Services, County Criminal Justice Profiles; U.S. Bureau of the Census, City and County Databook (1970); California Bureau of Finance (unpublished mimeographs).

*p<.05   **p<.01   ***p<.001

pears when inequality and crime are controlled separately. These findings appear to indicate that where inequality is greater, court caseloads will also be greater, despite police resource levels. The relationship between police resources and actual court caseload pressure appears to be explained by inequality in the population. As shown earlier, in table 7, inequality may lead to increased police resources, which, in turn, may lead to higher reported crime rates.

The partial correlations in table 12 are consistent with these findings as they relate to court caseload. Inequality explains away the relation between police resources and court caseload (it affects both). It also explains the relation between crime and caseload pressure but is likely to be associated with crime mainly through its effect on police resource levels. While causal priority is not established here, or in any studies to date, it is interesting to note that inequality may affect court caseload pressure independent of police resources and is only slightly reduced when crime rate is controlled. This appears to document the institutionalized selection process of authorities, which results in heavy concentrations of minority defendants.

Table 13 shows the partial correlations among demographic characteristics, original guilty pleas, and the rate of prison sentencing. Poverty remains positively related to the rate of prison sentencing when other variables are controlled. Unemployment and original guilty pleas also remain positively related, although they are reduced

TABLE 12 Court Caseload Pressure by Inequality, Police Resources, and
Felony Crime Rate 1970 (Partial Correlations)

| | | Police | Police | Felony |
Controls (N=20)	Inequality	Spending	Personnel	Crime Rate
Inequality	---	.09	.02	-.15
Police Spending	.59*	---	---	.12
Police Personnel	.56*	---	---	.14
Felony Crime Rate	.30	.15	.25	---

Sources: Bureau of Criminal Statistics and Special Services, County Criminal Justice
           Profiles; U.S. Bureau of the Census, City and County Databook (1970).

*p<.01

TABLE 13 Rate of Prison Sentencing by Selected Independent and Control
Variables 1970 (Partial Correlations)

	Independent Variables			
	Original			Percent
Controls (N=33)	Guilty Plea	Poverty	Unemployment	Urban
Original Guilty Plea	---	.37*	.22	-.06
Poverty	.22	---	.20	0
Unemployment	.23	.39**	---	-.06
Percent Urban	.27	.42**	.26	---

Sources: Bureau of Criminal Statistics and Special Services, County Criminal Justice
          Profiles; U.S. Bureau of the Census, City and County Databook (1970).

*p<.05   **p<.01

slightly from their original degrees of association (.42 and .39 respectively). In contrast, the original negative relation between urbanization and prison sentencing ($-.32$) is reduced to zero. Of all demographic characteristics measured, poverty shows the highest association with prison sentencing.

SUMMARY

The foregoing analysis has uncovered some interesting possible configurations of factors that bear on the system capacity model of crime and punishment. It must be noted, however, that these findings are tentative at best, since the analysis considers three variable relations only and is based on aggregate data. This makes inferences concerning causality problematic. Thus, the results presented here are meant to be more suggestive than definitive.

The findings reveal the complex set of interrelationships among crime, law, and society. The goal of this analysis has been to begin to disentangle these relationships. Figure 13 displays the patterns uncovered by this analysis, and a possible causal configuration of the main variables of interest. The deterrence relationship is included (sentencing affecting crime), since it cannot be entirely discarded on

FIGURE 13 Observed Interrelationships among Main Variables
and Possible Causal Configuration

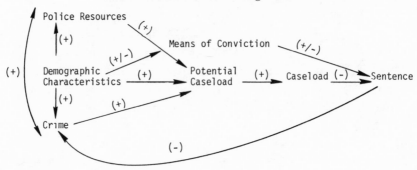

the basis of this (or any other) analysis. This relationship, however, was relatively minor given other potential influences in the overall "crime rate system."

Inequality, measured by the percent of black people in the population, may be an important determinant of police resource levels, which, in turn, are related to rates of reported felony crime. This measure of inequality also appears to explain the original association found between police resources and caseload pressure. There is also evidence to suggest that inequality in the population influences potential court caseload independent of other measured demographic characteristics.

The original finding of no significant associations between measures of caseload and means of conviction remains when demographic variables are controlled. Of all demographic characteristics measured, poverty remains significantly related to prison sentencing when controls are added.

The possible influence of inequality on police resource levels and potential and actual court caseload points to the importance of this population characteristic when examining crime and punishment. The results indicate that inequality may be more of a positive influence on police resources than a source of increased rates of reported crime. Police resources are more closely related to rates of reported crime than are any of the demographic characteristics measured. Inequality remains significantly related to police resources even when the rate of reported crime is controlled. The relation between inequality and reported crime virtually "disappears," however, when police resources are controlled. Thus, the findings indicate that inequality and police resources are related *regardless* of the rate of reported crime. While this analysis establishes no temporal priority between these two factors, it seems more plausible that the percent of black people in the population might affect resource levels of the police, rather than that police resources might affect inequality.

Police resources and inequality are also related to both potential and actual court caseload, which, in turn, appear to influence criminal sentencing. Caseload pressure does not seem to influence criminal sentencing by generating a higher rate of plea bargaining, or a greater degree of "assembly-line justice." Rather, as discussed earlier, heavier caseloads in courts may affect the qualitative aspects of plea bargains (e.g., "going rates") and result in lowered penalties for convicted defendants. The theoretical and policy implications of these and other findings are discussed in the following chapter.

VIII. Conclusion

This study has examined the aggregate relations among crime, demographic characteristics, criminal justice resources, court processing, and final sanctioning outcomes at the court level. It has attempted to identify the macrosociological relationships that exist among these social phenomena. The findings can only be generalized at the county level, since individual cases were not examined.

The implications for deterrence theory and research are clear from the findings. Current criminal justice practices, especially the extremely low probability of certain and severe punishment, indicate that the deterrent efficacy of punishment is likely to be minimal. This is not to say that deterrence does not or cannot work, but only that it is highly unlikely under present practices of criminal justice. In addition, this study examines probability of sanction at the court level only. Other aspects of sanctioning have not been examined. The results presented here are positive enough, however, to at least question current research on deterrence, in that there appear to be many more identifiable relationships present in the etiology of crime and punishment than merely an effect of punishment on crime. Court caseloads, influenced particularly by the degree of inequality in the population, appear to be pushing down formal penalty structures, and hence the probability of sanction. The inability of courts to produce severe and certain sanctions is also linked to the overfunding of police relative to other criminal justice agencies, especially the office of the prosecutor. Putting more cops on the beat may lead to a further erosion of the deterrent efficacy of punishment, as more violators are pushed through the "revolving door" of the courts. What defendants actually see as capricious and arbitrary practices in criminal courts can only lead to a further disrespect for law among those in the lower class who comprise the vast majority of cases in felony courts.[1] In view of rather

104

uncertain sanctions, and contempt for the process by which they are applied, the reality of deterrence as an effect of punishment is extremely limited for those the system aspires to deter the most—the lower class. In the words of Rusche and Kirchheimer:

> The crime rate can really be influenced only if society is in a position to offer its members a certain measure of security and to guarantee a reasonable standard of living. The shift from a repressive penal policy to a progressive program can then be raised out of the sphere of humanitarianism to constructive social activity. . . . The futility of severe punishment and cruel treatment may be proven a thousand times, but so long as society is unable to solve its social problems, repression, the easy way out, will always be accepted.[2]

The role of the police in the generation of crime and punishment cannot be underestimated. In studying the ineffectiveness of increased police personnel to prevent crime, Levine notes:

> To the extent that potential criminals correctly perceive the limitations of police, the credibility of legal sanctions is diminished and the deterrent capacity of the criminal justice system is undermined.[3]

In addition to this proposition, the findings of this study indicate that a similar phenomenon is likely operating at the felony court level. The extremely low probability of severe sanctioning in court may further undermine deterrent goals of punishment. Violators who are processed through the system may become cynical of the criminal law after exposure to what might readily be perceived as arbitrary court practices, undermining a major tenet of the deterrence doctrine, according to Andenaes,[4] namely, the legitimacy of the legal system. Thus, the irregular and minimal imposition of criminal sanctions by courts is likely to add to the ineffectiveness of increased police to prevent crime. Moreover, the data reported here indicate that less certain sanctioning occurs precisely in those areas that have higher police capacity in terms of resources per capita.

The results reported here are also congruent with those found by Wellford.[5] In analyzing crime rates, socioeconomic variables, and police resources, Wellford finds that socioeconomic variables account for 59 percent of the variation in crime rate, whereas "crime control" variables account for only 6 percent. This finding was seen as indicative of the incapacity of police to deal with the "crime problem."

In contrast to the findings of a study conducted by Atkinson and Dunn,[6] who claim that 60 percent of the variation in police resources is explained by crime rate, the results presented in this study indicate that this may be misleading. Inequality remains significantly related to police resources when crime rate is controlled. Thus, *regardless* of crime, where inequality is high, police resources are likely to be high. When police resources are controlled, the relationship between inequality and crime is dramatically reduced, indicating the possible intervening influence of police capacity in the relation between inequality and reported crime. This finding is also at odds with a study by McPheters and Stronge.[7] Using simultaneous equations to disentangle the mutual effects of crime and police resources, they chose an identification restriction that indicates that demographic characteristics are causally related to crime but do not influence police resources independently. That is, it is assumed that demographic characteristics influence police resources *only* through their effects on crime. The results presented here indicate that inequality may influence police resources *independent* of its effect on crime, thus questioning their main underlying assumption.

Finally, the results related to caseloads and adversariness do not support the notion that caseloads are responsible for increased rates of plea bargaining. Caseloads do appear to reduce the certainty of severe sentencing outcomes in felony courts, but this does not seem to be brought about by less adversariness in the processing of cases.

This is contrary to the argument set forth by Blumberg, who posits that increased caseloads lead to less adversariness in the processing of criminal cases. He states:

> The seeming separateness of the parties (police, prosecution, judge, probation officer, psychiatrist, defense counsel, and accused) is illusory. On the contrary, these "adversaries" are integrated into a bureaucratic matrix. They are a functional system, eliminating any "separateness" that may have existed. The very fact that the parties are not independent helps to weaken the idea of truth through combat.[8]

The results reported here question Blumberg's position that criminal justice agencies are integrated into a "bureaucratic matrix." While some degree of cooperation is sure to exist, the data show that, as of 1974, prolonged bargaining had become the norm in California counties. In addition, criminal justice agencies receive funds from different sources, and the vast differences in resources among agencies suggest that they are not very well integrated into a "system." There is no formal hierarchy of authority in criminal justice; each agency, although somewhat dependent on the activities of other agencies, is an independent organizational entity. Furthermore, although some cooperation exists between agencies, Skolnick notes that this does "not demonstrably impede the quality of representation."[9]

There is little doubt that formal goals of punishment, including that of deterrence, may become secondary to personal and administrative goals of participants in the legal process. However, this does not necessarily mean that less adversariness will result. Rather, what the findings here indicate is a "demise of statutory punishment." Caseloads appear less responsible for declining adversariness in felony courts than for a reduction in criminal punishments. The resources of the court appear to be saturated by the cases brought before it. That the adversary ideal is not met in each and every case does not imply that there is no adversariness at all in the adjudication of criminal cases.[10] Moreover, in this study, as well as in others,[11] there is no clear evidence found that indicates that caseloads influence the rapid processing of cases.

It is presently impossible for the state to administer sanctions that are both swift and severe to the vast majority of criminal defendants. This nonpractice stands in direct opposition to the major tenets of deterrence doctrine. It appears more plausible that rates of crime, influenced by inequality, other socioeconomic conditions, and overfunding of police relative to courts and prisons, have pushed down formal penalty structures. This does not disprove deterrence, but merely documents that its effects, if they exist at all, are likely to be greatly reduced in practice. Thus, the task for future research should not be to determine whether deterrence in the abstract is capable of working, but rather whether deterrence is likely to operate given the practices and structure of American criminal justice.

POLICY IMPLICATIONS

This study indicates that the more violators we put into the criminal justice system, the less capable it becomes in effecting crime control through deterrence. At the same time, we know that the crime problem is growing. If people are to advocate putting increased resources into the criminal justice system, they cannot argue this on the grounds that it will deter crime. If there are other grounds they wish to argue, those can be studied in turn. The results presented here indicate that deterrence is not a valid basis for increasing criminal justice resources or for pouring more money into the "fight against crime."

The foregoing analysis presents quite a different picture of crime and punishment, and one that can help inform crime control policies. The policy relevance of a system capacity perspective on criminal justice may not seem readily apparent. This is the case for two basic reasons. First, it questions the increasingly common idea that government manipulation of the legal machinery alone is effective in controlling crime. Second, and just as important, if there is a "capacity issue" that must be dealt with in formulating crime control policy, how should it be considered? Should we increase resources for official agencies, or attempt other methods to curb the flow of crime? There are no easy answers to such questions. Nevertheless, they need to be addressed in order to understand the implications of system capacity for crime control policy.

In a recent newspaper article, well-known commentator on crime and criminal justice James Q. Wilson notes the following about "rehabilitating" the country's prison system:

> There are no inexpensive solutions to the problem. Politicians and voters who complain loudly about crime and then vote against higher expenditures for correctional facilities are being irresponsible. We cannot go on packing more persons into inadequate facilities—even if our consciences will permit it, federal judges will not.[12]

Wilson's thoughts about the "inadequacies" of present facilities as well as the response by judges seem in line with a system capacity approach. His solutions to the problem entail "more responsibility" on the part of legislators and voters, in addition to better means of both managing and screening offenders, and the construction of more and better prisons. It is doubtful, however, that such an approach will, by itself, effect any significant degree of crime control. The amount of prison construction needed to decently house existing prisoners, to say nothing of additional ones in the future, is simply not possible given huge budget deficits at federal, state, and local levels. Without attention to the social conditions that breed crime, and thereby produce the work flows for criminal justice agencies, such an approach would likely be doomed to failure, even ignoring the fact that public monies are largely nonexistent. Caseloads would deny the possibility of deterrence.

Wilson is aware that this may indeed be true, and even argues the case in his influential work, *Thinking About Crime.*

> When thousands of felony cases must be settled each year in a court, there are overpowering pressures to settle them on the basis of plea bargaining in order to avoid the time and expense of a trial. The defendant is offered a reduced charge or a lighter sentence in exchange for a plea of guilty. Though congested dockets are not the only reason for this practice, an increase in congestion increases the incentives for such bargaining and thus may increase the proportion of lighter sentences. For those who believe in the deterrence theory of sentencing, it is a grim irony: The more crime increases, the more the pressure on court calendars, and the greater the chances that the response to the crime increase will be a sentence decrease.[13]

This idea is pushed to the background as Wilson argues that another reason for this pattern has to do with the belief of many judges that prison sentences are futile. Even if this is the case, however, it is still a capacity issue. If prisons were not so overcrowded and ineffective in reforming criminals, judges would likely feel differently. Nine pages later, Wilson argues that the probability of punishment should be increased in order to deter and incapacitate criminals, which is at odds with his statements concerning the "grim irony" facing those trying to effect deterrence through sentencing.

Wilson's logic concerning crime control policy is largely misleading. In yet another passage of the same book, he argues that we must increase resources for criminal justice sanctioning, after he acknowledges the influence of poverty, unemployment, and inequality in producing crime. He notes:

> To a degree, anticrime policies may be frustrated by the failure of unemployment policies, but it would be equally correct to say that so long as the criminal justice system does not impede crime, efforts to reduce unemployment will not work. If legitimate opportunities for work are unavailable, many young persons will turn to crime; but if criminal opportunities are profitable, many young persons will not take those legitimate jobs that exist. The benefits of work and the costs of crime must be increased simultaneously; to increase one but not the other makes sense only if one assumes that young people are irrational.[14]

Wilson is largely incorrect in this analysis. He ignores a central point in looking at the "costs" of crime. By increasing legitimate job opportunities and *genuinely* enhancing the benefits of work, the costs of crime will be driven up naturally, without increased resources for criminal justice. If this aspect of social inequality is reduced, and it is clearly demonstrated that legitimate and profitable opportunities are desirable and geared toward upward social mobility, the criminal justice system would be under less strain and have a greater capacity to process violators. Many middle and upper class persons choose legitimate jobs for precisely these reasons, even though they too could "profit more" from illegal activity. Unemployment, discrimination, and inequality must be reduced if the criminal justice system is to help effect crime control. This is a positive approach to controlling crime, not one that relies on negative sanctions to force people into submitting to inequitable and miserable conditions.

Building more prisons and expanding criminal justice resources may seem like "reasonable," "common sense" responses to the crime problem. Yet, not unlike many "common sense" notions, one does not have to look very far to uncover inherent contradictions.

A rather clear example of this is offered by Elliot Currie,[15] who examines the sardonic nature of the politics of crime control in his critique of the Reagan administration's Task Force on Violent Crime. After pointing out that the Task Force "acknowledged" that violent crime reflected breakdowns in various social networks and institutions, Currie notes:

> . . . the Task Force went on to say that it hadn't concerned itself with any of those possible causes, partly because its mandate was to explore what the Justice Department, not "government" as a whole, could do about crime, but also because "we are not convinced that a government, by the invention of new programs or the management of existing institutions, can by itself recreate those familial and neighborhood conditions, those social opportunities and those personal values that in all likelihood are the prerequisites of tranquil communities." The task force was "mindful of the risks of assuming that the government can solve whatever problem it addresses."
>
> The Task Force's sense of the "limits to what government can do," however, didn't stop it from proposing a variety of government interventions into criminal justice policy.[16]

First, as Currie astutely observes, why a study group concerned with controlling "violent crime" must limit its approach to only what the Department of Justice can do is indeed curious, if not dangerous and counterproductive. Such a stance clearly limits the scope of possible interventions to increasing the size of the criminal justice system and the state's control over the individual. This "get tough" stance on crime by policy makers is doomed to failure because of prohibitive costs and the fact that it has not yet been conclusively demonstrated that increasing control resources while ignoring conditions that breed crime will serve to reduce crime rates. Rather, there is every indication that as criminal justice resources grow, so does the crime problem. Increasing the state's capacity to punish is simply not enough to effect crime control. It is an expensive and negative proposal that will fail unless concommitant efforts are made to improve social conditions, reintegrate communities, and reduce discrimination and inequality in the population. Such efforts have never been attempted on a large scale, or over a time period long enough to allow a reasonable evaluation of results. That current policy makers are simply "unconvinced" by such social interventions is a premature judgment, based less on facts and more on political considerations. Indeed, the evidence already suggests that building more prisons and putting more people behind bars is not an effective solution to crime control. Within the past ten years the number of state and federal prisoners increased by about 50 percent, yet rates of violent crimes have continued to climb. The United States incarcerates people at a higher rate than any other advanced country in the world (with very few exceptions that people would feel comfortable being compared to) and still manages to enjoy the highest violent crime rate. Can the message be *any clearer* that there are "things" that can affect crime other than merely punishment?

Even assuming for the moment that increasing punishment through new prison construction could reduce crime, how much would have to be spent? Reagan's Task Force estimated $2 billion. This figure is largely misleading and likely to be in serious error. A National Institute of Justice study showed that as of 1978 it would cost between $8 and $10 billion in prison construction costs alone just to house the *existing* prison population under decent conditions. Further evidence of the unrealistic and misleading nature of the Reagan Task Force figure is demonstrated by Currie, who uses the Task Force's own estimate of per inmate construction and annual operating resources to describe the likely costs of further prison construction.

On January 1, 1981, there were about 300,000 inmates in state and federal prisons. Tripling that population, to aim, say, at a 20 percent reduction in "index" crimes, would by these calculations, cost roughly $40 billion for construction alone, and add close to $8 billion annually in operating costs. We'd also need to vastly increase the funds we now put into state and local criminal expenditures, to accommodate the increased flow. As of 1978, even excluding police and state corrections, that was well over $6 billion a year.

All of this would assure us an incarceration rate ranging up to more than twenty times the rate prevailing in some Western European countries. It would still leave us with the highest rates of serious violent crimes in the developed world.[17]

Even calculating costs on a more conservative basis would produce projected expenditures well over the $2 billion figure put forth by Reagan's Task Force and, more importantly, would *not guarantee any* reduction in serious crime. Moreover, with serious budget deficits at both state and federal levels, there are few, if any, sources for enormous increases in criminal justice expenditures to begin with. This preceding scenario also ignores the important fact that even if such resources were found, they would necessarily be generated at the expense of other positive domestic functions.

The foregoing analysis does not claim that prisons aren't necessary, or that certain individuals shouldn't be incarcerated. It simply questions the current vision that society should opt for protectors with the biggest guns and prisons at their disposal. When policy makers and the public come to fully realize that what they presently do about crime (as well as other social problems) is usually first an issue of politics and second a matter of reason, science, and humanity, perhaps then the largest hurdle will be cleared to producing effective social interventions that can measurably increase the quality of life.

The criminal justice system is likely to work best when it is used least. It should not be used routinely, but exceptionally. With this major tenet as a focus for criminal justice and crime control policy, perhaps we can start to attack crime at its real sources, and allow the criminal justice system to operate effectively. Our modern system of criminal justice was born from a radical social movement in Europe two centuries ago. Perhaps it is time to seriously reexamine criminological premises and provide new directions for the future.

APPENDIX 1 Felony Crime Rates per 100,000 Population
Median, Semi-Interquartile Range (Q), First (Q₁) and Third (Q₃) Quartiles
California Counties 1966–1974

Crime Rates	1966	1967	1968	1969	1970	1971	1972	1973	1974	Percentage Change
Total Felony Crime[a]										
Median	1605.6	1668.6	1902.3	2162.3	2505.9	2774.8	2835.0	2983.8	3288.8	104.8
(Q)	398.0	358.3	403.4	444.4	507.5	529.1	530.5	420.7	459.6	
(Q₁)	1239.8	1388.7	1641.3	1848.1	2103.5	2446.7	2496.9	2531.7	2791.9	
(Q₃)	2035.7	2105.3	2448.1	2736.8	3118.4	3504.9	3557.8	3373.1	3711.0	
Number of Counties	(25)	(24)	(24)	(24)	(25)	(25)	(25)	(27)	(27)	
Felony Property Crime[b]										
Median	1507.7	1567.0	1800.0	2041.1	2365.4	2573.1	2575.0	2727.0	2924.4	94.0
(Q)	378.2	319.5	382.8	435.0	469.8	507.9	451.5	330.4	416.8	
(Q₁)	1167.2	1306.7	1537.3	1729.3	1946.1	2290.3	2326.0	2356.1	2549.8	
(Q₃)	1923.6	1945.9	2302.9	2599.3	2886.7	3306.0	3229.0	3016.8	3383.4	
Number of Counties	(25)	(24)	(24)	(24)	(25)	(25)	(25)	(27)	(27)	
Felony Personal Crime[c]										
Median	113.6	120.3	123.4	137.5	153.3	181.2	193.8	243.6	303.1	166.8
(Q)	32.0	29.2	27.7	21.3	26.5	38.8	48.7	64.9	72.8	
(Q₁)	82.7	89.0	95.0	118.4	126.7	150.6	164.5	190.6	201.3	
(Q₃)	146.6	147.3	150.3	160.9	179.7	228.2	261.8	320.3	346.8	
Number of Counties	(25)	(25)	(25)	(25)	(25)	(25)	(25)	(27)	(27)	

Source: Bureau of Criminal Statistics and Special Services, County Criminal Justice Profiles.

[a] Includes willful homicide, rape, assault, robbery, burglary, theft, and auto theft.
[b] Includes robbery, burglary, theft, and auto theft.
[c] Includes willful homicide, rape, and assault.

APPENDIX 2 Criminal Justice Spending Per Capita
Median, Semi-Interquartile Range (Q), First (Q₁), and Third (Q₃) Quartiles
California Counties 1968–1974)

Spending	1968	1969	1970	1971	1972	1973	1974	Percentage Change
Police								
Median	15.9	17.8	19.4	22.0	23.8	26.7	30.6	92.6
(Q)	1.7	1.9	2.1	2.9	3.3	3.9	5.0	
(Q₁)	13.9	16.1	17.8	19.2	21.2	23.9	26.6	
(Q₃)	17.3	19.8	21.9	25.0	27.8	31.6	36.6	
Number of Counties	(58)	(58)	(58)	(58)	(58)	(58)	(58)	
Prosecutorial								
Median	1.5	1.7	2.0	2.3	2.6	2.9	3.4	126.7
(Q)	.4	.3	.3	.4	.5	.5	.6	
(Q₁)	1.2	1.4	1.7	2.0	2.2	2.6	2.9	
(Q₃)	1.9	2.0	2.3	2.8	3.2	3.5	4.0	
Number of Counties	(54)	(54)	(54)	(55)	(55)	(55)	(56)	
Superior Court								
Median	1.0	1.1	1.1	1.2	1.3	1.4	1.5	50.0
(Q)	.3	.3	.4	.4	.5	.6	.7	
(Q₁)	.8	.8	.8	.9	1.0	1.1	1.1	
(Q₃)	1.3	1.4	1.6	1.7	1.9	2.0	2.4	
Number of Counties	(58)	(58)	(58)	(58)	(58)	(58)	(58)	

Source: Bureau of Criminal Statistics and Special Services, County Criminal Justice Profiles.

APPENDIX 3 Criminal Justice Personnel per 100,000 Population
Median, Semi-Interquartile Range (Q), First (Q₁) and Third (Q₃) Quartiles
California Counties 1968–1974

Personnel	1968	1969	1970	1971	1972	1973	1974	Percentage Change
Police								
Median	181	192	196	202	208	224	227	25.4
(Q)	24	30	26	27	28	27	29	
(Q₁)	162	173	180	183	192	196	203	
(Q₃)	210	233	231	241	247	250	261	
Number of Counties	(56)	(56)	(56)	(56)	(56)	(56)	(56)	
Prosecutorial								
Median	--	16	17	17	19	21	22	37.5
(Q)	--	4	5	4	5	4	3	
(Q₁)	--	13	12	14	15	19	20	
(Q₃)	--	21	22	22	25	26	26	
Number of Counties	--	(56)	(48)	(55)	(54)	(57)	(56)	
Superior Court								
Median	2.7	2.6	2.7	2.7	2.8	2.9	2.8	3.7
(Q)	1.8	1.6	1.5	1.3	1.2	1.2	1.2	
(Q₁)	2.0	2.1	2.2	2.3	2.3	2.3	2.2	
(Q₃)	5.6	5.3	5.1	4.8	4.6	4.6	4.6	
Number of Counties	(55)	(57)	(57)	(57)	(57)	(57)	(57)	

Source: Bureau of Criminal Statistics and Special Services, County Criminal Justice Profiles.

APPENDIX 4 Superior Court Means of Conviction
Median, Semi-Interquartile Range (Q), First (Q_1) and Third (Q_3) Quartiles California Counties 1966–1973

Means of Conviction[a]	1966	1967	1968	1969	1970	1971	1972	1973	Percentage Change
Original Guilty Pleas									
Median	.62	.44	.53	.53	.49	.45	.41	.39	-37.1
(Q)	.10	.07	.11	.07	.13	.13	.13	.14	
(Q_1)	.50	.42	.42	.36	.33	.30	.27	.21	
(Q_3)	.70	.56	.64	.63	.59	.56	.52	.49	
Number of Counties	(55)	(27)	(53)	(55)	(55)	(56)	(55)	(56)	
Changed Guilty Pleas									
Median	.27	.39	.33	.36	.40	.44	.47	.47	74.1
(Q)	.09	.07	.11	.11	.11	.12	.14	.16	
(Q_1)	.17	.29	.23	.24	.29	.33	.32	.33	
(Q_3)	.34	.43	.44	.45	.51	.57	.59	.64	
Number of Counties	(51)	(27)	(53)	(54)	(55)	(55)	(55)	(56)	
Trials in Which Defendant Found Guilty									
Median	.13	.15	.12	.11	.11	.10	.10	.12	-7.7
(Q)	.05	.02	.03	.04	.04	.03	.03	.03	
(Q_1)	.09	.11	.09	.08	.09	.07	.08	.09	
(Q_3)	.18	.15	.15	.16	.16	.13	.13	.15	
Number of Counties	(53)	(27)	(53)	(53)	(50)	(54)	(55)	(55)	

Source: Bureau of Criminal Statistics and Special Services, County Criminal Justice Profiles.

[a] Expressed as proportion of all convictions.

APPENDIX 5 Superior Court Level of Conviction
Median, Semi-Interquartile Range (Q), First (Q_1) and Third (Q_3) Quartiles
California Counties 1966–1973

Level of Conviction[a]	1966	1967	1968	1969	1970	1971	1972	1973	Percentage Change
Felony									
Median	.68	.72	.69	.66	.67	.70	.76	.79	16.2
(Q)	.09	.08	.09	.13	.12	.12	.14	.10	
(Q_1)	.59	.64	.59	.50	.56	.54	.58	.63	
(Q_3)	.76	.80	.77	.76	.80	.77	.85	.83	
Number of Counties	(55)	(27)	(54)	(55)	(55)	(55)	(55)	(56)	
Misdemeanor									
Median	.32	.28	.30	.34	.33	.30	.24	.21	-34.4
(Q)	.09	.08	.09	.12	.12	.12	.14	.08	
(Q_1)	.22	.19	.23	.23	.20	.22	.15	.17	
(Q_3)	.40	.35	.40	.46	.43	.45	.43	.33	
Number of Counties	(55)	(27)	(54)	(55)	(56)	(55)	(55)	(56)	

Source: Bureau of Criminal Statistics and Special Services, County Criminal Justice Profiles.

[a]Expressed as proportion of all convictions

Appendix 6 Superior Court Sentencing
Median, Semi-Interquartile Range (Q), First (Q$_1$) and Third (Q$_3$) Quartiles
California Counties 1966–1973

Sentencing[a]	1966	1967	1968	1969	1970	1971	1972	1973	Percentage Change
Prison									
Median	.29	.22	.18	.16	.16	.13	.15	.15	-48.3
(Q)	.09	.06	.05	.06	.06	.04	.05	.05	
(Q$_1$)	.17	.16	.15	.10	.11	.10	.09	.11	
(Q$_3$)	.34	.28	.25	.21	.22	.18	.18	.21	
Number of Counties	(55)	(27)	(53)	(55)	(53)	(53)	(54)	(55)	
Probation									
Median	.23	.24	.24	.23	.26	.28	.26	.26	13.0
(Q)	.11	.09	.10	.10	.09	.11	.10	.09	
(Q$_1$)	.15	.15	.16	.16	.18	.17	.18	.17	
(Q$_3$)	.36	.33	.36	.36	.36	.38	.37	.35	
Number of Counties	(54)	(27)	(54)	(54)	(54)	(55)	(55)	(55)	
Probation with Jail									
Median	.20	.32	.33	.33	.33	.35	.36	.37	85.0
(Q)	.09	.11	.10	.12	.12	.12	.10	.10	
(Q$_1$)	.12	.20	.22	.18	.22	.23	.26	.27	
(Q$_3$)	.29	.41	.42	.42	.46	.46	.46	.47	
Number of Counties	(54)	(27)	(52)	(55)	(55)	(55)	(55)	(55)	
Jail Only									
Median	.15	.09	.13	.12	.11	.08	.08	.08	-46.7
(Q)	.06	.04	.04	.07	.06	.05	.05	.04	
(Q$_1$)	.10	.06	.07	.06	.05	.06	.04	.04	
(Q$_3$)	.22	.14	.19	.19	.17	.16	.14	.12	
Number of Counties	(52)	(27)	(50)	(54)	(53)	(54)	(54)	(52)	

Source: Bureau of Criminal Statistics and Special Services, County Criminal Justice Profiles.

[a]Expressed as a proportion of all convictions. Sentences not shown include California Youth Authority, fine, mental hygiene, and California Rehabilitation Center for narcotics addicts.

APPENDIX 7 Potential and Actual Court Caseload
Median, Semi-Interquartile Range (Q), First (Q_1) and Third (Q_3) Quartiles
California Counties 1966–1974

Caseload	1966	1967	1968	1969	1970	1971	1972	1973	1974	Percentage Change
Dispositions per Capita										
Median	1.63	1.61	1.75	2.06	2.26	2.52	2.43	2.36	--	45.0
(Q)	.42	.28	.45	.64	.43	.68	.55	.57	--	
(Q_1)	1.20	1.29	1.43	1.79	1.88	1.85	1.87	1.85	--	
(Q_3)	2.17	1.85	2.32	3.06	2.74	3.21	2.97	2.99	--	
Number of Counties	(45)	(27)	(48)	(48)	(45)	(49)	(50)	(46)	--	
Police-Prosecutor Resource Imbalance[a]										
Median	--	--	9.67	9.31	8.94	9.18	9.02	9.15	9.11	-6.0
(Q)	--	--	2.65	2.37	1.67	1.95	1.86	2.02	1.40	
(Q_1)	--	--	7.45	7.69	7.88	7.56	7.46	6.85	7.13	
(Q_3)	--	--	12.74	12.42	11.62	11.46	11.17	10.89	9.93	
Number of Counties	--	--	(54)	(54)	(54)	(55)	(55)	(55)	(56)	

Felony Arrest Rate per 100,000										
Median	412.6	442.1	533.8	616.5	721.6	814.0	864.4	903.3	1062.0	157.4
(Q)	62.7	69.6	95.8	125.0	93.1	135.5	169.2	156.2	122.8	
(Q1)	334.0	395.7	455.5	529.2	677.7	713.2	723.7	750.7	964.6	
(Q3)	459.4	534.8	647.0	781.1	853.8	984.1	1062.1	1063.1	1210.2	
Number of Counties	(27)	(26)	(26)	(27)	(26)	(27)	(28)	(28)	(28)	
Actual Caseload[b]										
Median	--	--	--	13.6	12.9	15.8	12.6	10.7	--	-21.3
(Q)	--	--	--	5.1	5.9	5.2	4.4	3.6	--	
(Q1)	--	--	--	10.1	9.3	10.6	9.8	8.3	--	
(Q3)	--	--	--	20.2	21.2	21.0	18.5	15.5	--	
Number of Counties	--	--	--	(47)	(39)	(47)	(47)	(46)	--	

Source: Bureau of Criminal Statistics and Special Services, County Criminal Justice Profiles.

[a]Measured by the ratio of police to prosecutor personnel.

[b]Measured by the ratio of dispositions per prosecutor personnel (Superior and Municipal Courts).

NOTES

Chapter One

1. R. Pound, *Criminal Justice in America* (New York: DaCapo Press, [1930] 1975), 68–69.

2. R. Martinson, "What Works? Questions and Answers about Prison Reform," *Public Interest* 12 (1974):22–55.

3. For a discussion of issues related to criminal punishment and retribution in particular, see E. van den Haag, *Punishing Criminals: Concerning a Very Old and Painful Question* (New York: Basic Books, 1975). For a recent debate on just deserts, see J. Braithwaite, "Challenging Just Deserts: Punishing White-Collar Criminals," *The Journal of Criminal Law and Criminology* 73 (1982):723–63; and E. van den Haag, "The Criminal Law as a Threat System," *The Journal of Criminal Law and Criminology* 73 (1982):769–85; replies by the authors are also included in the journal.

4. A. von Hirsch, *Doing Justice: The Choice of Punishments* (New York: Hill and Wang, 1976).

5. See J. Braithwaite, "Paradoxes of Class Bias in Criminological Research," in *Rethinking Criminology*, ed. H. E. Pepinsky (Beverly Hills: Sage Publications, 1982), 61–84.

6. J. Bentham, *An Introduction to the Principles of Morals and Legislation* (New York: Hafner [1825] 1973); C. Beccaria, *Essay on Crimes and Punishment*, translated by E. Ingraham (Palo Alto: Academic Reprints [1764] 1953).

7. See F. E. Zimring, *Perspectives on Deterrence* (Washington, D.C.: NIMH, 1971); F. E. Zimring and G. J. Hawkins, *Deterrence: The Legal Threat in Crime Control* (Chicago: University of Chicago Press, 1973); J. P. Gibbs, *Crime, Punishment and Deterrence* (New York: Elsevier, 1975); idem, "Social Control, Deterrence, and Perspectives on Social Order," *Social Forces* 56 (1977):408–23.

8. See Pound, *Criminal Justice*.

9. H. N. Pontell, "Deterrence: Theory versus Practice," *Criminology* 16 (1978):3–22.

10. D. Nagin, "Crime Rates, Sanction Levels, and Constraints on Prison Population," *Law and Society Review* 12 (1978):341–66.

11. M. Geerken and W. R. Gove, "Deterrence: Some Theoretical Considerations," *Law and Society Review* 9 (1975):497–513; idem, "Deterrence, Overload, and Incapacitation: An Empirical Evaluation," *Social Forces* 56 (1977):424–47.

12. L. Phillips and H. L. Votey, Jr., "An Economic Analysis of the Deterrent Effect of Law Enforcement on Criminal Activity," *Journal of Criminal Law, Criminology and Police Science* 63 (1972):330–42; C. H. Logan, "Arrest Rates and Deterrence," *Social Science Quarterly* 56 (1975):376–89; R. Shinnar and S. Shinnar, "The Effects of the Criminal Justice System on the Control of Crime: A Quantitative Approach," *Law and Society Review* 9 (1975):581–611.

13. J. Braithwaite, *Crime, Inequality and Social Policy* (London: Routledge and Kegan Paul, 1979).

Chapter Two

1. For recent and comprehensive reviews of the literature see Gibbs, *Crime, Punishment and Deterrence;* A. Blumstein, J. Cohen, and D. Nagin, eds., *Deterrence and Incapacitation: Estimating the Effects of Criminal Sanctions on Crime Rates* (Washington, D.C.: National Academy of Sciences, 1978); and C. R. Tittle, *Sanctions and Social Deviance: The Question of Deterrence* (New York: Praeger, 1980).

2. W. J. Chambliss, "The Deterrent Influence of Punishment," *Crime and Delinquency* 12 (1966):70–75.

3. G. H. Mead, "The Psychology of Punitive Justice," *American Journal of Sociology* 23 (1918):577–602.

4. J. Andenaes, "General Prevention—Illusion or Reality?" *Journal of Criminal Law, Criminology and Police Science* 43 (1952):176–98; idem, "The General Preventive Effects of Punishment," *University of Pennsylvania Law Review* 114 (1966):949–83; idem, *Punishment and Deterrence* (Ann Arbor: University of Michigan Press, 1974); idem, "General Prevention Revisited: Research and Policy Implications," *Journal of Criminal Law and Criminology* 66 (1975):338–65.

5. Zimring and Hawkins, *Deterrence.*

6. Gibbs, *Crime, Punishment and Deterrence.*

7. G. P. Waldo and T. G. Chiricos, "Perceived Penal Sanction and Self-reported Criminality: A Neglected Approach to Deterrence Research," *Social Problems* 19 (1972):522–40.

8. R. L. Henshel and R. A. Silverman, eds., *Perception in Criminology* (New York: Columbia University Press, 1975).

9. M. L. Erickson, J. P. Gibbs, and G. F. Jensen, "The Deterrence Doctrine and the Perceived Certainty of Legal Punishments," *American Sociological Review* 42 (1977):305–17.

10. H. G. Grasmick and G. J. Bryjak, "The Deterrent Effect of Perceived Severity of Punishment," *Social Forces* 59 (1980):471–91.

11. General prevention is a term Andenaes (1952) uses to include the moralizing, educative, habit building, as well as the threatening effects of the criminal law and its operation. He conceives it to be a broader term than "mere deterrence," which he uses to denote the strictly threatening aspect of law.

12. D. Miller, A. Rosenthal, D. Miller, and S. Ruzek, "Deterrent Effects of Criminal Sanctions," Progress Report of the California Assembly Committee on Criminal Procedure, Sacramento (1968).

13. Ibid.

14. Andenaes, "General Prevention," 179–80.

15. See G. Becker, "Crime and Punishment: An Economic Approach," *Journal of Political Economy* 78 (1967):526–36; and I. Ehrlich, "Participation in Illegitimate Activities: A Theoretical and Empirical Investigation," *Journal of Political Economy* 81 (1973):521–65.

16. Andenaes, "General Prevention," 179.

17. Ibid., 180.

18. C. D. Stone, *Where the Law Ends: The Social Control of Corporate Behavior* (New York: Harper and Row, 1975), 35.

Chapter Three

1. Andenaes, "General Preventive Effects of Punishment," 953.

2. See C. R. Tittle and C. H. Logan, "Sanctions and Deviance: Evidence and Remaining Questions," *Law and Society Review* 7 (1973):371–92; Zimring and Hawkins, *Deterrence;* Gibbs, *Crime, Punishment and Deterrence;* M. Silberman, "Toward a Theory of Criminal Deterrence," *American Sociological Review* 41 (1976):442–61; Blumstein, Cohen, and Nagin, eds., *Deterrence and Incapacitation;* Tittle, *Sanctions and Social Deviance.*

3. See Zimring and Hawkins, *Deterrence.*

4. See F. Tannenbaum, *Crime and the Community* (New York: Columbia University Press, 1938); H. E. Barnes and N. Teeters, *New Horizons in Criminology* (Englewood Cliffs: Prentice-Hall, 1959); and T. Sellin, *The Death Penalty* (Philadelphia: American Law Institute, 1959).

5. See note 2 above.

6. J. P. Gibbs, "Crime, Punishment and Deterrence," *Southwestern Social Science Quarterly* 48 (1968):515–30.

7. Ibid., 529–30.

8. B. Schwartz, "The Effect in Philadelphia of Pennsylvania's Increased Penalties for Rape and Attempted Rape," *Journal of Criminal Law, Criminology and Police Science* 59 (1968):509–15.

9. Ibid., 514.

10. L. N. Gray and J. D. Martin, "Punishment and Deterrence: Another Analysis of Gibbs' Data," *Social Science Quarterly* 50 (1969):389–95.

11. Ibid., 394.

12. F. D. Bean and R. G. Cushing, "Criminal Homicide, Punishment and Deterrence: Methodological and Substantive Reconsiderations," *Social Science Quarterly* 52 (1971):277–89.

13. Ibid., 286.

14. M. E. Wolfgang, "A Sociological Analysis of Criminal Homicide," *Federal Probation* 25 (1961):48–55.

15. Bean and Cushing, "Criminal Homicide, Punishment and Deterrence," 289.

16. C. R. Tittle, "Crime Rates and Legal Sanctions," *Social Problems* 16 (1969): 409–23.

17. Ibid., 417.

18. Ibid., 419.

19. Ibid.

20. T. G. Chiricos and G. P. Waldo, "Punishment and Crime: An Examination of Some Empirical Evidence," *Social Problems* 18 (1970):200–17.

21. Ibid., 208.

22. Ibid.

23. See G. V. Fuguitt and S. Lieberson, "Correlation of Ratios on Different Scores Having Common Terms," in *Sociological Methodology 1973–1974*, ed. H. L. Costner (San Francisco: Jossey-Bass, 1974), 128–44.

24. Chiricos and Waldo, "Punishment and Crime," 213.

25. C. H. Logan, "On Punishment and Crime (Chiricos and Waldo 1970): Some Methodological Commentary," *Social Problems* 19 (1971):280–84.

26. Ibid., 283.

27. Ibid.
28. C. H. Logan, "General Deterrent Effects of Imprisonment," *Social Forces* 51 (1972):64–73.
29. Ibid., 73.
30. S. Kobrin, S. G. Lubeck, E. W. Hansen, and R. Yeaman, "The Deterrent Effectiveness of Criminal Justice Sanction Strategies," Final Report to the National Institute of Law Enforcement and Criminal Justice, Washington, D.C. (1972).
31. C. R. Tittle and A. R. Rowe, "Certainty of Arrest and Crime Rates: A Further Test of the Deterrence Hypothesis," *Social Forces* 52 (1974): 455–62.
32. Ibid., 459.
33. Blumstein, Cohen, and Nagin, *Deterrence and Incapacitation.*
34. J. D. Casper, *American Criminal Justice: The Defendant's Perspective* (Englewood Cliffs: Prentice-Hall, 1972).
35. Ehrlich, "Participation in Illegitimate Activities."
36. Blumstein, Cohen, and Nagin, *Deterrence and Incapacitation.*
37. Ibid., 40.
38. For a discussion of other difficulties in causal modeling with aggregate data, see Hirschi and Selvin's treatment of Lander's work in T. Hirschi and H. C. Selvin, *Principles of Survey Analysis* (New York: Free Press, 1973).
39. Blumstein, Cohen, and Nagin, *Deterrence and Incapacitation*, 42.
40. A. Cohen, *Deviance and Control* (Englewood Cliffs: Prentice-Hall, 1966).
41. Pound, *Criminal Justice.*
42. Tittle, "Crime Rates and Legal Sanctions," 420.
43. This has been accomplished in recent work by Nagin, "Crime Rates, Sanction Levels and Constraints on Prison Population"; Pontell, "Deterrence"; and D. F. Greenberg, R. C. Kessler, and C. H. Logan, "A Panel Model of Crime Rates and Arrest Rates," *American Sociological Review* 44 (1979):843–50.
44. See G. F. Jensen, "Crime Doesn't Pay: Correlates of a Shared Misunderstanding," *Social Problems* 17 (1969):189–201; and J. Toby, "Deterrence without Punishment," *Criminology* 19 (1981):195–209.

Chapter Four

1. A. S. Blumberg, *Criminal Justice* (Chicago: Quadrangle, 1967); and H. James, *Crisis in the Courts* (New York: David McKay, 1968).
2. A. Blumstein and J. Cohen, "A Theory of the Stability of Punishment," *Journal of Criminal Law and Criminology* 64 (1973):198–207.
3. See Pontell, "Deterrence," 12.
4. For a discussion of issues and literature related to the interaction of crime, caseloads, and punishment, see H. N. Pontell, "System Capacity and Criminal Justice: Theoretical and Substantive Considerations," in *Rethinking Criminology*, ed. H. E. Pepinsky (Beverly Hills: Sage Publications, 1982), 131–43.
5. Blumberg, *Criminal Justice.*
6. See J. H. Skolnick, "Social Control in the Adversary System," *Journal of Conflict Resolution* 11 (1967):52–70; and G. F. Cole, "The Decision to Prosecute," *Law and Society Review* 4 (1970):313–43.

7. M. M. Feeley, "Two Models of the Criminal Justice System: An Organizational Perspective," *Law and Society Review* 7 (1973):407–25.

8. Blumberg, *Criminal Justice*, 22.

9. Ibid.

10. M. Mileski, "Courtroom Encounters: An Observation Study of a Lower Criminal Court," *Law and Society Review* 5 (1971): 473–538.

11. Skolnick, "Social Control"; and Cole, "Decision to Prosecute."

12. L. M. Mather, "Some Determinants of the Method of Case Disposition: Decision-making by Public Defenders in Los Angeles," *Law and Society Review* 8 (1973):187.

13. See Feeley, "Two Models"; idem, "The Effects of Heavy Caseloads," paper presented at the annual meeting of the American Political Science Association, San Francisco, September 1975; idem, *The Process is the Punishment: Handling Cases in a Lower Criminal Court* (New York: Russell Sage Foundation, 1979); M. Heumann, "A Note on Plea Bargaining and Case Pressure," *Law and Society Review* 9 (1975):515–28; idem, *Plea Bargaining: The Experiences of Prosecutors, Judges and Defense Attorneys* (Chicago: University of Chicago Press, 1978); P. F. Nardulli, *The Courtroom Elite: An Organizational Perspective on Criminal Justice* (Cambridge, Mass.: Ballinger Publishing Co., 1978); idem, "The Caseload Controversy and the Study of Criminal Courts," *Journal of Criminal Law and Criminology* 70 (1979): 89–101.

14. See H. L. Packer, *The Limits of the Criminal Sanction* (Palo Alto: Stanford University Press, 1968).

15. Ibid., 159.

16. See Feeley, "Two Models."

17. A. Etzioni, "Two Approaches to Organizational Analysis: A Critique and a Suggestion," *Administrative Science Quarterly* 5 (1960): 257–78.

18. Ibid., 263.

19. Feeley, "Two Models," 409.

20. Ibid.

21. Ibid., 412.

22. Ibid., 413.

23. See Pontell, "System Capacity."

24. Feeley, "Two Models," 413.

25. Skolnick, "Social Control," 55.

Chapter Five

1. For a discussion of the idea of "crime rate system," see R. L. Henshel, "Considerations on the Deterrence and System Capacity Models," *Criminology* 16 (1978):35–46.

2. See M. Fleming, *The Price of Perfect Justice* (New York: Basic Books, 1974).

3. Blumstein, Cohen, and Nagin, *Deterrence and Incapacitation;* Nagin, "Crime Rates"; and Pontell, "Deterrence."

4. I. D. Balbus, *The Dialectics of Legal Repression: Black Rebels Before the American Criminal Courts* (New York: Transaction Books, 1977).

5. J. P. Levine, "The Ineffectiveness of Adding Police to Prevent Crime," *Public Policy* 23 (1975): 523–45.

6. President's Commission on Law Enforcement and Administration of

Justice, *The Challenge of Crime in a Free Society* (Washington, D.C.: Government Printing Office, 1967a).

7. Levine, "Ineffectiveness of Adding Police."

8. A. J. Reiss, Jr., "Discretionary Justice," in *Handbook of Criminology*, ed. D. Glaser (Chicago: Rand McNally, 1974), 690.

9. Mather, "Case Disposition," 192.

10. President's Commission on Law Enforcement and Administration of Justice, *The Courts* (Washington, D.C.: Government Printing Office, 1967b).

11. See Nagin, "Crime Rates"; and Pontell, "Deterrence."

12. See W. A. Bonger, *Criminality and Economic Conditions* (Bloomington: Indiana University Press [1916], 1969); J. Braithwaite, *Crime, Inequality and Social Policy;* R. Quinney, *Class, State and Crime: On the Theory and Practice of Criminal Justice* (New York: David McKay, 1977); G. M. Sykes, *Criminology* (New York: Harcourt, Brace and Jovanovich, 1978); and M. E. Wolfgang, "Urban Crime," in *The Metropolitan Enigma*, ed. J. Q. Wilson (Cambridge, Mass.: Harvard University Press, 1968), 245–81.

13. See D. J. Black, "Production of Crime Rates," *American Sociological Review* 35 (1970):733–48; M. J. Greenwood and W. J. Wadycki, "Crime Rates and Public Expenditures for Police Protection: Their Interaction," *Review of Social Economy* 31 (1973):232–41; C. R. Huff and J. M. Stahura, "Police Employment and Suburban Crime," *Criminology* 17 (1980):461–70; H. Jacob and M. J. Rich, "The Effects of the Police on Crime: A Second Look," *Law and Society Review* 15 (1980–81):109–22; Levine, "Ineffectiveness of Adding Police"; H. E. Pepinsky, *Crime Control Strategies: An Introduction to the Study of Crime Control* (New York: Oxford University Press, 1980).

14. See G. Rusche and O. Kirchheimer, *Punishment and Social Structure* (New York: Columbia University Press, 1939).

15. N. Christie, "Changes in Penal Values," *Scandinavian Studies in Criminology* 2 (1968):161–72.

16. Rusche and Kirchheimer, *Punishment and Social Structure.*

17. Ibid.

18. Christie, "Penal Values."

19. Ibid., 172.

20. A good review of the literature on judicial decision making is given by M. Levin, *Urban Politics and the Criminal Courts* (Chicago: University of Chicago Press, 1977).

21. J. Hagan, "Extra-Legal Attributes and Criminal Sentencing: An Assessment of a Sociological Viewpoint," *Law and Society Review* 8 (1974): 357–83; and J. Hagan, I. H. Nagel (Bernstein), and C. Albonetti, "The Differential Sentencing of White-Collar Offenders in Ten Federal District Courts," *American Sociological Review* 45 (1980): 802–20.

22. K. Mann, S. Wheeler, and A. Sarat, "Sentencing the White-Collar Offender," *American Criminal Law Review* 17 (1980):479–500.

23. P. H. Rossi, E. Waite, C. E. Bose, and R. E. Berk, "The Seriousness of Crimes: Normative Structure and Individual Differences," *American Sociological Review* 39 (1974): 224–37.

24. Mann, Wheeler, and Sarat, "White-Collar Offender."

25. Braithwaite, *Crime, Inequality and Social Policy.*

26. Rusche and Kirchheimer, *Punishment and Social Structure.*

27. Blumstein and Cohen, "Stability of Punishment."

28. President's Commission, *Challenge of Crime.*

29. See James, *Crisis in the Courts;* Packer, *Criminal Sanction;* Casper, *American Criminal Justice;* and L. Downie, Jr., *Justice Denied: The Case for Reform of the Courts* (New York: Praeger, 1971).

30. See G. L. Geis, "Statistics Concerning Race and Crime," *Crime and Delinquency* 11 (1965):142–50; R. Quinney, *The Problem of Crime* (New York: Dodd, Mead, 1975).

31. W. G. Skogan, "The Validity of Official Crime Statistics: An Empirical Investigation," *Social Science Quarterly* 55 (1974):25–38.

32. See Black, "Production of Crime Rates"; H. E. Pepinsky, *Crime and Conflict: A Study of Law and Society* (New York: Academic Press, 1976a); idem, "Police Offense-Reporting Behavior," *Journal of Research in Crime and Delinquency* 13 (1976b):33–47; idem, "Stereotyping as a Force for Increasing Crime Rates," *Law and Human Behavior* 1 (1977):290–308; idem, *Crime Control Strategies;* J. H. Skolnick, *Justice Without Trial: Law Enforcement in Democratic Society* (New York: John Wiley and Sons, 1966); and J. Q. Wilson, *Varieties of Police Behavior: The Management of Law and Order in Eight Communities* (New York: Atheneum, 1968).

33. Geis, "Statistics," 145.

34. J. I. Kitsuse and A. V. Cicourel, "A Note on the Uses of Official Statistics," *Social Problems* 11 (1963):131–39.

35. P. F. Lazarsfeld and H. Menzel, "On the Relation between Individual and Collective Properties," in *A Sociological Reader on Complex Organizations,* ed. A. Etzioni (New York: Holt, Rinehart and Winston, 1961), 499–516.

36. J. W. Meyer and B. Rowan "Institutionalized Organizations: Formal Structure as Myth and Ceremony," *American Journal of Sociology* 83 (1977):351.

37. Pepinsky, *Crime Control Strategies.*

38. Demographic data were only available for the year 1970.

39. Since demographic data were not available for years other than 1970, ecological associations were examined for that year alone.

40. An excellent discussion of this data source as well as aggregate level data analysis is given in S. Kobrin et al., "Deterrent Effectiveness."

41. State of California, Department of Justice, Bureau of Criminal Statistics and Special Services, *County Criminal Justice Profiles, 1975* (Sacramento: State of California, Department of Justice, 1975).

Chapter Six

1. U.S. Department of Justice, LEAA, *Criminal Justice Statistics Sourcebook, 1976* (Washington, D.C.: Government Printing Office).

2. Ibid.

3. Mather, "Case Disposition."

4. Blumberg, *Criminal Justice;* Mather, "Case Disposition."

5. Ibid.

6. L. M. Mather, "The Outsider in the Courtroom: An Alternative Role for the Defense," in *The Potential for Reform of Criminal Justice,* ed. H. Jacob (Beverly Hills: Sage Publications, 1974), 263–89.

7. Ibid.

8. State of California, Department of Justice, Bureau of Criminal Statistics

and Special Services, *Crime and Delinquency in California, 1970* (Sacramento: State of California, Department of Justice, 1970), 122.

9. Mather, "Case Disposition."

10. See Appendix 7.

Chapter Seven

1. A recent study has found that the relative size of minority population serves as a good indicator of the degree of social inequality. The authors state: "In terms of the objectives of the research, the most important conclusion is that the relative size of minority population emerges as a robust predictor of inequality." P. W. Frisbie and L. Neidert, "Inequality and the Relative Size of Minority Populations: A Comparative Analysis, *American Journal of Sociology* 82 (1977):1029.

2. See Greenwood and Wadycki, "Crime Rates"; Jacob and Rich, "Effects of Police"; Levine, "Ineffectiveness of Adding Police"; L. R. McPheters and W. B. Stronge, "Law Enforcement Expenditures and Urban Crime," *National Tax Journal* 27 (1974):633–44; Pepinsky, "Police Offense-Reporting"; idem, "Stereotyping"; idem, *Crime Control Strategies.*

3. Ibid.

4. See Levine, "Ineffectiveness of Adding Police"; and G. L. Kelling, *The Kansas City Preventive Patrol Experiment: A Summary Report* (Washington, D.C.: The Police Foundation, 1974).

5. See Mather, "Case Disposition."

6. See President's Commission, *The Courts.*

7. See Blumberg, *Criminal Justice.*

8. See Skolnick, "Social Control"; Feeley, "Two Models"; and P. Utz, *Settling the Facts: Discretion and Negotiation in Criminal Court* (Lexington, Mass.: D. C. Heath, 1978).

9. See The Cleveland Foundation, *Criminal Justice in Cleveland* (The Cleveland Foundation, 1921); Heumann, "Note on Plea Bargaining"; and idem, *Plea Bargaining.*

10. Unfortunately, these data were not available for the present study.

11. Utz, *Settling the Facts.*

12. Mather, "Case Disposition."

13. Downie, *Justice Denied.*

14. Rusche and Kirchheimer, *Punishment and Social Structure.*

15. Christie, "Penal Values."

16. Nagin,"Crime Rates"; Pontell, "Deterrence."

17. The use of regression techniques is problematic here because of both the high interrelationships among the proposed independent variables and the small number of cases (counties). This is usually handled by excluding one, or some, of the highly related variables or by using factor analysis to reduce the number of variables in an equation. Both of these solutions were considered unsatisfactory in the present situation, since the point of interest is precisely the possible effects of each variable on court caseloads and criminal justice processing. The small number of counties on which the regressions would be based also dictated that fewer variables be analyzed in the same equation. Partial correlation analysis provides an adequate statistical alternative for this exploratory analysis, as it measures the correlation of residuals

between the independent and dependent variables after the effects of a third ("control") variable have been removed. Thus, while it is understood that partial correlations are of limited analytic value compared to regressions, they appear better suited to the present exploratory analysis.

18. For a general discussion and criticism of using *any* statistical methodology for conducting a causal analysis with aggregate data, see H. C. Selvin's analysis of the work of Bentzel and Hansen in "On Following in Someone's Footsteps," in *Qualitative and Quantitative Social Research: Papers in Honor of Paul F. Lazarsfeld,* ed. R. K. Merton (New York: Free Press, 1979), 232–44.

19. See note 2 above.

Chapter Eight

1. See Casper, *American Criminal Justice;* and C. E. Silberman, *Criminal Violence, Criminal Justice* (New York: Random House, 1978).

2. Rusche and Kirchheimer, *Punishment and Social Structure,* 207.

3. Levine, "Ineffectiveness of Adding Police," 531.

4. Andenaes, "General Prevention."

5. C. R. Wellford, "Crime and the Police: A Multivariate Analysis," *Criminology* 12 (1974):195–213.

6. D. N. Atkinson and J. A. Dunn, Jr., "The Impact of Expenditures on the Operation of the Criminal Justice System," *Washburn Law Journal* 12 (1973):269–80.

7. McPheters and Stronge, "Law Enforcement."

8. Blumberg, *Criminal Justice,* 181.

9. Skolnick, "Social Control," 53.

10. See Utz, *Settling the Facts.*

11. See Feeley, "Heavy Caseloads"; Heumann, "Note on Plea Bargaining"; idem, *Plea Bargaining;* Mather, "Case Disposition"; Mileski, "Courtroom Encounters"; Nardulli, *Courtroom Elite;* and idem, "Caseload Controversy."

12. J. Q. Wilson, "Rehabilitating Our Prisons," *Family Weekly,* Sunday, 15 Nov. 1981:4.

13. J. Q. Wilson, *Thinking about Crime* (New York: Basic Books, 1975), 166–67.

14. Ibid., 202.

15. E. Currie, "Crime and Ideology," *Working Papers* 9 (1982):26–35.

16. Ibid., 27.

17. Ibid., 35.

SELECTED BIBLIOGRAPHY

Aldrich, H. E., and J. Pfeffer. 1976. Environments of organizations. *Annual Review of Sociology* 2:79–105.

Alschuler, A. W. 1968. The prosecutor's role in plea bargaining. *University of Chicago Law Review* 36:50–112.

Andenaes, J. 1952. General prevention—illusion or reality? *Journal of Criminal Law, Criminology and Police Science* 43:176–98.

———. 1966. The general preventive effects of punishment. *University of Pennsylvania Law Review* 114:949–83.

———. 1974. *Punishment and deterrence.* Ann Arbor: University of Michigan Press.

———. 1975. General prevention revisited: Research and policy implications. *Journal of Criminal Law and Criminology* 66:338–65.

Antunes, G., and A. L. Hunt. 1973. The deterrent impact of criminal sanctions: Some implications for criminal justice policy. *Journal of Urban Law* 51:145–61.

Atkinson, D. N., and J. A. Dunn, Jr. 1973. The impact of expenditures on the operation of the criminal justice system. *Washburn Law Journal* 12:269–80.

Bailey, W. C., and R. W. Smith. 1972. Punishment: Its severity and certainty. *Journal of Criminal Law, Criminology and Police Science* 63:530–39.

Balbus, I. D. 1977. *The dialectics of legal repression: Black rebels before the American criminal courts.* New York: Transaction Books.

Ball, J. C. 1955. The deterrence concept in criminology and law. *Journal of Criminal Law, Criminology and Police Science* 46:347–54.

Barnes, H. E., and N. Teeters. 1959. *New horizons in criminology.* Englewood Cliffs: Prentice-Hall.

Bean, F. D., and R. G. Cushing. 1971. Criminal homicide, punishment and deterrence: Methodological and substantive reconsiderations. *Social Science Quarterly* 52:277–89.

Beccaria, C. [1764] 1953. *Essay on crimes and punishment.* Translated by E. Ingraham. Palo Alto: Academic Reprints.

Becker. G. 1967. Crime and punishment: An economic approach. *Journal of Political Economy* 78:526–36.

Bentham, J. [1825] 1973. *An introduction to the principles of morals and legislation.* New York: Hafner.

Bittner, E. 1967. The police on skid-row: A study of peace keeping. *American Sociological Review* 32:699–715.

Bittner, E., and A. Platt. 1966. The meaning of punishment. *Issues in Criminology* 2:79–99.

Black, D. J. 1970. Production of crime rates. *American Sociological Review* 35:733–48.

———. 1971. The social organization of arrest. *Stanford Law Review* 23:1087–1111.

Blumberg, A. S. 1967. *Criminal justice*. Chicago: Quadrangle.

Blumstein, A., and J. Cohen. 1973. A theory of the stability of punishment. *Journal of Criminal Law and Criminology* 64:198–207.

Blumstein, A., J. Cohen, and D. Nagin, eds. 1978. *Deterrence and incapacitation: Estimating the effects of criminal sanctions on crime rates*. Washington, D.C.: National Academy of Sciences.

Bohrnstedt, G. W. 1969. Observations on the measurement of change. In *Sociological methodology*, ed. E. F. Borgatta, 113–33. San Francisco: Jossey-Bass.

Bonger, W. A. [1916] 1969. *Criminality and economic conditions*. Bloomington: Indiana University Press.

Bordua, D. J., and E. W. Haurek. 1970. The police budget's lot. *American Behavioral Scientist* 13:667–80.

Braithwaite, J. 1979. *Crime, inequality and social policy*. London: Routledge and Kegan Paul.

———. 1982a. Paradoxes of class bias in criminological research. In *Rethinking criminology*, ed. H. E. Pepinsky, 61–84. Beverly Hills: Sage Publications.

———. 1982b. Challenging just deserts: Punishing white-collar criminals. *The Journal of Criminal Law and Criminology* 73:723–63.

State of California, Department of Justice. Bureau of Criminal Statistics and Special Services. *County criminal justice profiles, 1975*. Sacramento: State of California, Department of Justice.

———. *Crime and delinquency in California, 1970*. Sacramento: State of California, Department of Justice.

Carlin, J. E., and J. Howard. 1965. Legal representation and class justice. *UCLA Law Review*, 12:381–437.

Casper, J. D. 1972. *American criminal justice: The defendant's perspective*. Englewood Cliffs: Prentice-Hall.

Chambliss, W. J. 1966. The deterrent influence of punishment. *Crime and Delinquency* 12:70–75.

Chiricos, T. G., and G. P. Waldo. 1970. Punishment and crime: An examination of some empirical evidence. *Social Problems* 18:200–17.

Christie, N. 1968. Changes in penal values. *Scandinavian Studies in Criminology* (Oslo: Universitetsforlaget) 2:161–72.

The Cleveland Foundation. 1921. *Criminal Justice in Cleveland*. Cleveland: The Cleveland Foundation.

Cohen, A. 1966. *Deviance and control*. Englewood Cliffs: Prentice-Hall.

Cole, G. F. 1970. The decision to prosecute. *Law and Society Review* 4:313–43.

Cousineau, D. F. 1973. A critique of the ecological approach to the study of deterrence. *Social Science Quarterly* 54:152–58.

Crockett, G. W., Jr. 1972. Racism in the courts. *Howard Law Journal* 17:296–99.

Currie, E. 1982. Crime and ideology. *Working Papers* 9:26–35.

Downie, L., Jr. 1971. *Justice denied: The case for reform of the courts*. New York: Praeger.

Ehrlich, I. 1973. Participation in illegitimate activities: A theoretical and empirical investigation. *Journal of Political Economy* 81:521–65.

Enker, A. 1967. *Perspectives on plea bargaining*. President's Commission on Law

Enforcement and the Administration of Justice. Task Force Report: The Courts. Washington, D.C.: Government Printing Office.

Erickson, M. L., and J. P. Gibbs. 1975. Specific versus general properties of legal punishments and deterrence. *Social Science Quarterly* 56:390–97.

Erickson, M. L., J. P. Gibbs, and G. F. Jensen. 1977. The deterrence doctrine and the perceived certainty of legal punishments. *American Sociological Review* 42:305–17.

Etzioni, A. 1960. Two approaches to organizational analysis: A critique and a suggestion. *Administrative Science Quarterly* 5:257–78.

———. 1961. *A comparative analysis of complex organizations.* New York: Free Press.

Feeley, M. M. 1973. Two models of the criminal justice system: An organizational perspective. *Law and Society Review* 7:407–25.

———. 1975. The effects of heavy caseloads. Paper presented at the annual meeting of the American Political Science Association, San Francisco, September 1975.

———. 1979. *The process is the punishment: Handling cases in a lower criminal court.* New York: Russell Sage Foundation.

Fleming, M. 1974. *The price of perfect justice.* New York: Basic Books.

Frisbie, P. W., and L. Neidert. 1977. Inequality and the relative size of minority populations: A comparative analysis. *American Journal of Sociology* 82:1007–30.

Fuguitt, G. V., and S. Lieberson. 1974. Correlation of ratios on different scores having common terms. In *Sociological methodology 1973–1974,* ed. H. L. Costner, 128–44. San Francisco: Jossey-Bass.

Fuller, L. L. 1968. *Anatomy of the law.* New York: Mentor Books.

Geerken, M., and W. R. Gove. 1975. Deterrence: Some theoretical considerations. *Law and Society Review* 9:497–513.

———. 1977. Deterrence, overload, and incapacitation: An empirical evaluation. *Social Forces* 56:424–47.

Geis, G. L. 1965. Statistics concerning race and crime. *Crime and Delinquency* 11:142–50.

Gibbons, D. C. 1971. Observations on the study of crime causation. *American Journal of Sociology* 77:262–78.

Gibbs, J. P. 1968. Crime, punishment and deterrence. *Southwestern Social Science Quarterly* 48:515–30.

———. 1975. *Crime, punishment and deterrence.* New York: Elsevier.

———. 1977. Social control, deterrence, and perspectives on social order. *Social Forces* 56:408–23.

Goldstein, J. 1960. Police discretion not to invoke the criminal process: Low visibility decisions in the administration of justice. *Yale Law Journal* 69:543–94.

Grasmick, H. G., and G. J. Bryjak. 1980. The deterrent effect of perceived severity of punishment. *Social Forces* 59:471–91.

Gray, L. N., and J. D. Martin. 1969. Punishment and deterrence: Another analysis of Gibbs' data. *Social Science Quarterly* 50:389–95.

Greenberg, D. F., R. C. Kessler, and C. H. Logan. 1979. A panel model of crime rates and arrest rates. *American Sociological Review* 44:843–50.

Greenwood, M. J., and W. J. Wadycki. 1973. Crime rates and public expenditures for police protection: Their interaction. *Review of Social Economy* 31:232–41.

Hagan, J. 1974. Extra-legal attributes and criminal sentencing: An assessment of a sociological viewpoint. *Law and Society Review* 8:357–83.
Hagan, J., I. H. Nagel (Bernstein), and C. Albonetti, 1980. The differential sentencing of white-collar offenders in ten federal district courts. *American Sociological Review* 45:802–20.
Henshel, R. L. 1978. Considerations on the deterrence and system capacity models. *Criminology* 16:35–46.
Henshel, R. L., and R. A. Silverman, eds. 1975. *Perception in criminology.* New York: Columbia University Press.
Heumann, M. 1975. A note on plea bargaining and case pressure. *Law and Society Review* 9:515–28.
———. 1978. *Plea bargaining: The experiences of prosecutors, judges and defense attorneys.* Chicago: University of Chicago Press.
Heydebrand, W. V. 1977. The context of public bureaucracies: An organizational analysis of federal district courts. *Law and Society Review* 11:759–822.
Hirschi, T., and H. C. Selvin. 1973. *Principles of survey analysis.* New York: Free Press.
Hirst, P. 1972. Marx and Engels on law, crime and morality. *Economy and Society* 1:28–56.
Huff, C. R., and J. M. Stahura. 1980. Police employment and suburban crime. *Criminology* 17:461–70.

Jacob, H. 1972. *Justice in America: Courts, lawyers, and the judicial process.* 2nd ed. Boston: Little, Brown, and Co.
Jacob, H., and M. J. Rich, 1980–81. The effects of the police on crime: A second look. *Law and Society Review* 15:109–22.
James, H. 1968. *Crisis in the courts.* New York: David McKay.
Jensen, G. F. 1969. Crime doesn't pay: Correlates of a shared misunderstanding. *Social Problems* 17:189–201.

Kelling, G. L. 1974. *The Kansas City Prevention Patrol Experiment: A Summary Report.* Washington, D.C.: The Police Foundation.
Kitsuse, J. I., and A. V. Cicourel. 1963. A note on the uses of official statistics. *Social Problems* 11:131–39.
Kobrin, S., S. G. Lubeck, E. W. Hansen, and R. Yeaman. 1972. The deterrent effectiveness of criminal justice sanction strategies. Final Report to the National Institute of Law Enforcement and Criminal Justice. Washington, D.C.

Lazarsfeld, P. F., and H. Menzel. 1961. On the relation between individual and collective properties. In *A sociological reader on complex organizations,* ed. A. Etzioni, 499–516. New York: Holt, Rinehart and Winston.
Levin, M. 1977. *Urban politics and the criminal courts.* Chicago: University of Chicago Press.
Levine, J. P. 1975. The ineffectiveness of adding police to prevent crime. *Public Policy* 23:523–45.

Logan, C. H. 1971. On punishment and crime (Chiricos and Waldo 1970): Some methodological commentary. *Social Problems* 19:280–84.

———. 1972. General deterrent effects of imprisonment. *Social Forces* 51:64–73.

———. 1975. Arrest rates and deterrence. *Social Science Quarterly* 56:376–89.

———. 1978. Statistical artifacts in deterrence research. In *Quantitative studies in criminology*, ed. C. Wellford, 64–83. Beverly Hills: Sage Publications.

Mann, K., S. Wheeler, and A. Sarat. 1980. Sentencing the white-collar offender. *American Criminal Law Review* 17:479–500.

Mannheim, H., ed. 1960. *Pioneers in criminology.* Chicago: Quadrangle.

Martinson, R. 1974. What works? Questions and answers about prison reform. *Public Interest* 12:22–55.

Mather, L. M. 1973. Some determinants of the method of case disposition: Decision-making by public defenders in Los Angeles. *Law and Society Review* 8:187–211.

———. 1974. The outsider in the courtroom: An alternative role for the defense. In *The potential for reform of criminal justice*, ed. H. Jacob, 263–89. Beverly Hills: Sage Publications.

McPheters, L. R., and W. B. Stronge. 1974. Law enforcement expenditures and urban crime. *National Tax Journal* 27:633–44.

Mead, G. H. 1918. The psychology of punitive justice. *The American Journal of Sociology* 23:577–602.

Meir, R. F., and W. T. Johnson. 1977. Deterrence as social control: The legal and extralegal production of conformity. *American Sociological Review* 42:292–304.

Meyer, J. W., and B. Rowan. 1977. Institutionalized organizations: Formal structure as myth and ceremony. *American Journal of Sociology* 83:340–63.

Mileski, M. 1971. Courtroom encounters: An observation study of a lower criminal court. *Law and Society Review* 5:473–538.

Miller, D., A. Rosenthal, D. Miller, and S. Ruzek. 1968. Deterrent effects of criminal sanctions. Progress Report of the California Assembly Committee on Criminal Procedure. Sacramento, 1968.

Nagin, D. 1978. Crime rates, sanction levels, and constraints on prison population. *Law and Society Review* 12:341–66.

Nardulli, P. F. 1978. *The courtroom elite: An organizational perspective on criminal justice.* Cambridge, Mass.: Ballinger Publishing Co.

———. 1979. The caseload controversy and the study of criminal courts. *Journal of Criminal Law and Criminology* 70:89–101.

Newman, D. J. 1966. *Conviction: The determination of guilt or innocence without trial.* Boston: Little, Brown and Co.

O'Connor, J. 1973. *The fiscal crisis of the state.* New York: St. Martin's Press.

Packer, H. L. 1968. *The limits of the criminal sanction.* Palo Alto: Stanford University Press.

Pepinsky, H. E. 1976a. *Crime and conflict: A study of law and society.* New York: Academic Press.

————. 1976b. Police offense-reporting behavior. *Journal of Research in Crime and Delinquency* 13:33–47.

————. 1977. Stereotyping as a force for increasing crime rates. *Law and Human Behavior* 1:290–308.

————. 1980. *Crime control strategies: An introduction to the study of crime control.* New York: Oxford University Press.

Phillips, L., and H. L. Votey, Jr. 1972. An economic analysis of the deterrent effect of law enforcement on criminal activity. *The Journal of Criminal Law, Criminology and Police Science* 63:330–42.

Pontell, H. N. 1978. Deterrence: Theory versus practice. *Criminology* 16:3–22.

————. 1982. System capacity and criminal justice: Theoretical and substantive considerations. In *Rethinking criminology,* ed. H. E. Pepinsky, 131–43. Beverly Hills: Sage Publications.

Pound, R. [1930] 1975. *Criminal justice in America.* New York: DaCapo Press.

President's Commission on Law Enforcement and Administration of Justice. 1967a. *The challenge of crime in a free society.* Washington D.C.: Government Printing Office.

————. 1967b. *The courts.* Washington, D.C.: Government Printing Office.

Quinney, R. 1975. *The problem of crime.* New York: Dodd, Mead.

————. 1977. *Class, state and crime: On the theory and practice of criminal justice.* New York: David McKay.

Reasons, C. E., and J. L. Kuykendall, eds. 1972. *Race, crime, and justice.* Pacific Palisades, CA: Goodyear Publishing Co.

Reiss, A. J., Jr. 1974. Discretionary justice. In *Handbook of Criminology,* ed. D. Glaser, 679–99. Chicago: Rand McNally.

Rosett, A., and D. R. Cressey. 1976. *Justice by consent: Plea bargains in the American courthouse.* Philadelphia: J. B. Lippincott, Co.

Rossi, P. H., E. Waite, C. E. Bose, and R. E. Berk. 1974. The seriousness of crimes: Normative structure and individual differences. *American Sociological Review* 39:224–37.

Rothman, D. J. 1971. *The discovery of the asylum: Social order and disorder in the new republic.* Boston: Little, Brown and Co.

Rusche, G., and O. Kirchheimer. 1939. *Punishment and social structure.* New York: Columbia University Press.

Salem, R. G., and W. J. Bowers. 1970. Severity of formal sanctions as a deterrent to deviant behavior. *Law and Society Review* 5:21–40.

Schwartz, B. 1968. The effect in Philadelphia of Pennsylvania's increased penalties for rape and attempted rape. *Journal of Criminal Law, Criminology and Police Science* 59:509–15.

Scull, A. T. 1977. *Decarceration.* Englewood Cliffs, N.J.: Prentice-Hall.

Sellin, T. 1937. *Research memorandum on crime in the depression.* New York: Social Science Research Council.

————. 1959. *The death penalty.* Philadelphia: The American Law Institute.

Selvin, H. C. 1979. On following in someone's footsteps. In *Qualitative and quantitative social research: Papers in honor of Paul F. Lazarsfeld,* ed. R. K. Merton, 232–44. New York: Free Press.

Shinnar, R., and S. Shinnar. 1975. The effects of the criminal justice system on the control of crime: A quantitative approach. *Law and Society Review* 9:581–611.

Silberman, C. E. 1978. *Criminal violence, criminal justice.* New York: Random House.

Silberman, M. 1976. Toward a theory of criminal deterrence. *American Sociological Review* 41:442–61.

Skogan, W. G. 1974. The validity of official crime statistics: An empirical investigation. *Social Science Quarterly* 55:25–38.

Skolnick, J. H. 1966. *Justice without trial: Law enforcement in democratic society.* New York: John Wiley and Sons.

———. 1967. Social control in the adversary system. *Journal of Conflict Resolution* 11:52–70.

Stone, C. D. 1975. *Where the law ends: The social control of corporate behavior.* New York: Harper and Row.

Sudnow, D. 1965. Normal crimes: Sociological features of the penal code in a public defender office. *Social Problems* 12:255–76.

Sykes, G. M. 1978. *Criminology.* New York: Harcourt, Brace and Jovanovich.

Tannenbaum, F. 1938. *Crime and the community.* New York: Columbia University Press.

Tittle, C. R. 1969. Crime rates and legal sanctions. *Social Problems* 16:409–23

———. 1980. *Sanctions and social deviance: The question of deterrence.* New York: Praeger.

Tittle, C. R., and C. H. Logan. 1973. Sanctions and deviance: Evidence and remaining questions. *Law and Society Review* 7:371–92.

Tittle, C. R., and A. R. Rowe. 1973. Moral appeal, sanction threat, and deviance: An experimental test. *Social Problems* 20:488–98.

———. 1974. Certainty of arrest and crime rates: A further test of the deterrence hypothesis. *Social Forces* 52:455–62.

Toby, J. 1981. Deterrence without punishment. *Criminology* 19:195–209.

Tullock, G. 1974. Does punishment deter crime? *Public Interest* 36:103–11.

U. S. Department of Justice, LEAA. 1976. *Criminal Justice Statistics Sourcebook.* Washington, D.C.: Government Printing Office.

Utz, P. 1978. *Settling the facts: Discretion and negotiation in criminal court.* Lexington, Mass.: D. C. Heath.

van den Haag, E. 1975. *Punishing criminals: Concerning a very old and painful question.* New York: Basic Books.

———. 1982, The criminal law as a threat system. *The Journal of Criminal Law and Criminology* 73:769–85.

Vold, G. B. 1958. *Theoretical criminology.* New York: Oxford University Press.

von Hirsch, A. 1976 *Doing justice: The choice of punishments.* New York: Hill and Wang.

Waldo, G. P., and T. G. Chiricos. 1972. Perceived penal sanction and self-reported criminality: A neglected approach to deterrence research. *Social Problems* 19:522–40.

Wellford, C. R. 1974. Crime and the police: A multivariate analysis. *Criminology* 12:195–213.

Wilson, J. Q. 1968. *Varieties of police behavior: The management of law and order in eight communities*. New York: Atheneum.

———. 1975. *Thinking about crime*. New York: Basic Books.

———. 1981. Rehabilitating our prisons. *The Family Weekly*, 15 Nov. 1981, 4–8.

Wolfgang, M. E. 1961. A sociological analysis of criminal homicide. *Federal Probation* 25:48–55.

———. 1968. Urban crime. In *The metropolitan enigma*, ed. J. Q. Wilson, 245–81. Cambridge, Mass.: Harvard University Press.

Wright, E. O. 1973. *The politics of punishment: A critical analysis of prisons in America*. New York: Harper and Row.

Zimring, F. E. 1971. *Perspectives on deterrence*. Washington, D.C.: National Institute of Mental Health.

Zimring, F. E., and G. J. Hawkins. 1973. *Deterrence: The legal threat in crime control*. Chicago: University of Chicago Press.

INDEX